# LETTERHEAD + LOGO DESIGN 5

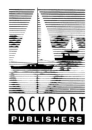

ROCKPORT PUBLISHERS
GLOUCESTER, MASSACHUSETTS

First published in the United States of America by:
Rockport Publishers, Inc.
33 Commercial Street
Gloucester, Massachusetts 01930-5089
Telephone: (978) 282-9590
Facsimile: (978) 283-2742

Distributed to the book trade and art trade in the United States by:
North Light Books, an imprint of
F & W Publications
1507 Dana Avenue
Cincinnati, Ohio 45207
Telephone: (800) 289-0963

Other Distribution by:
Rockport Publishers, Inc.
Gloucester, Massachusetts 01930-5089

ISBN 1-56496-405-1

10   9   8   7   6   5   4   3   2

Designer: Argus Visual Communication, Boston
Front Cover Images: left to right from top, p. 14, 19, 121, 122, 34, 28
Back Cover Images: p. 42, 136, 74
Printed in Hong Kong by Midas Printing Limited.

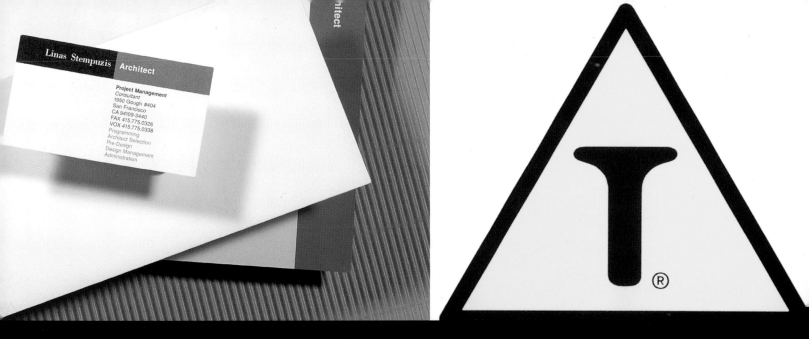

# LETTERHEAD + LOGO DESIGN ⑤

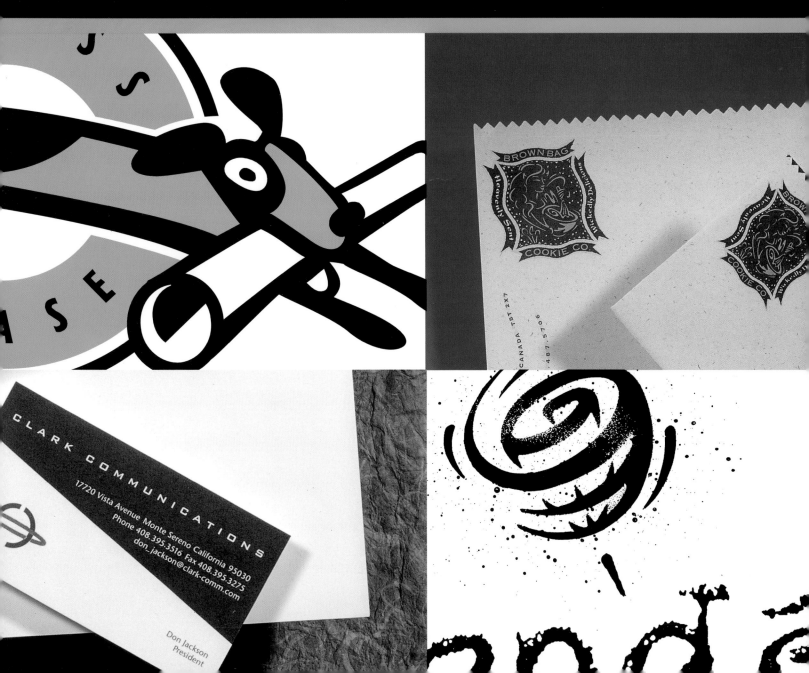

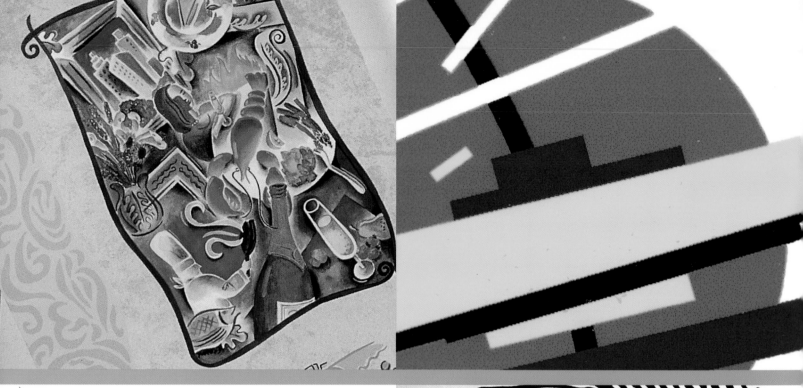

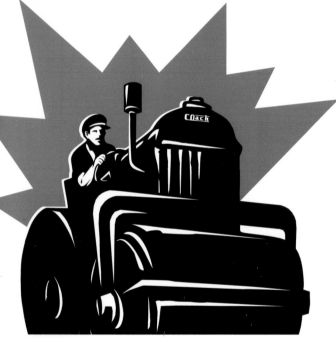

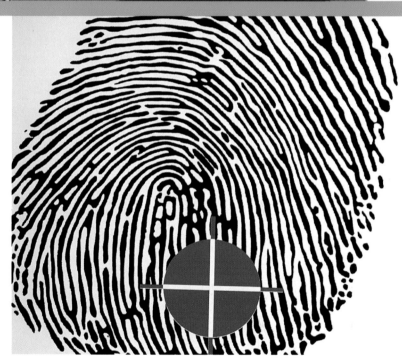

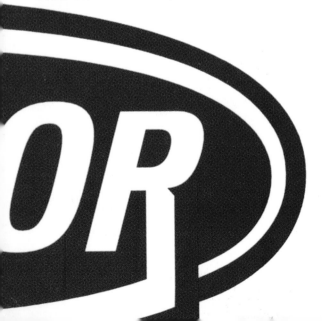

# CONTENTS

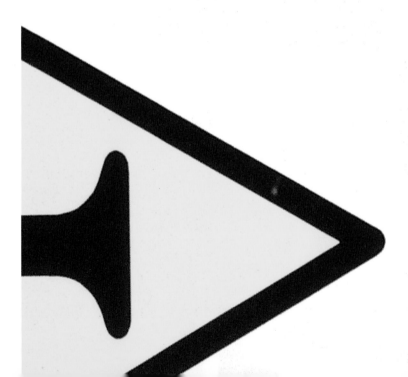

**DESIGN FIRM** | TRACY SABIN GRAPHIC DESIGN
**ART DIRECTOR** | ANDRÉ DUGGIN
**ILLUSTRATOR** | TRACY SABIN
**CLIENT** | YOU CAN SOAR, INC.
**TOOLS** | ADOBE ILLUSTRATOR

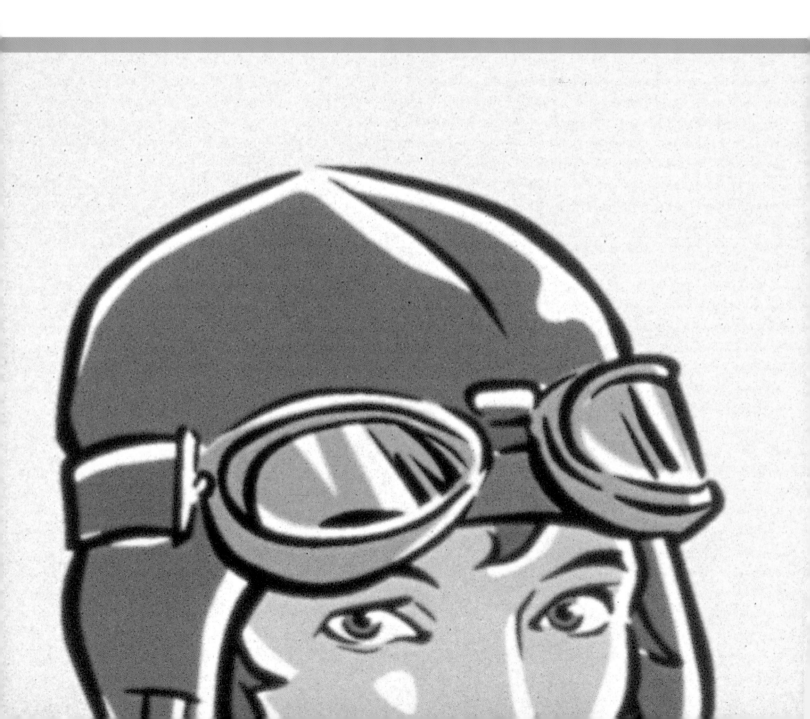

# INTRODUCTION

Who can deny the importance of a logo? A good brand identity will sell a product or confirm the legitimacy of any project. In designing this graphic element to be successful in the global marketplace, flexibility is key. A logo must translate on paper, over a fax, over the Internet, and be easily recognizable in every language. Colors and shapes must carefully be considered in order to effectively cross all cultural barriers. It must be timeless in its style and not be caught in current trends.

The logos presented in this book are exciting, new, and varied. Most have successfully met the requirements of a successful global design, others are on the way. While this book shows the logos presented on letterhead, it is clear that the business world is moving away from paper to electronic media.

Assuredly, the next volume in this collection will show more electronic examples of interactive logos, plus fantastic aspects that only the creative genius of the graphic design world could imagine.

ROY ALDEN, DESIGNER

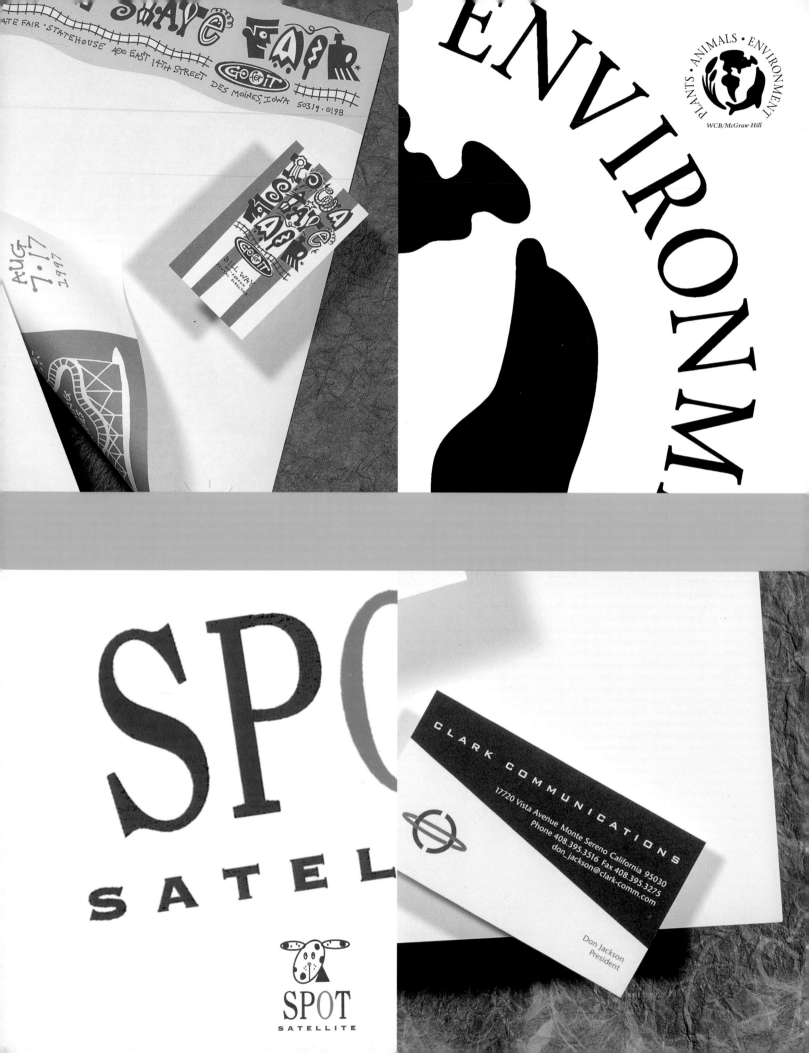

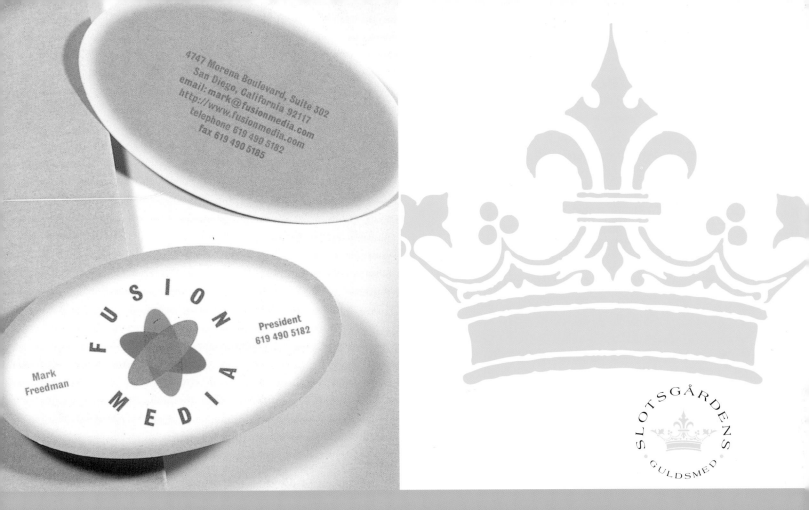

4747 Morena Boulevard, Suite 302
San Diego, California 92117
email: mark@fusionmedia.com
http://www.fusionmedia.com
telephone 619 490 5182
fax 619 490 5185

FUSION MEDIA

President
619 490 5182

Mark
Freedman

SLOTSGÅRDENS
GULDSMED

# PROFESSIONAL SERVICES

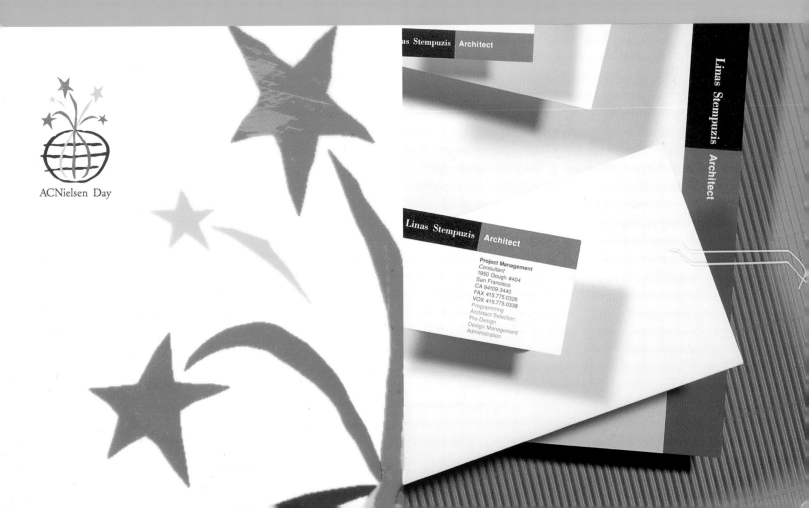

ACNielsen Day

Linas Stempuzis   Architect

Linas Stempuzis
Architect

Linas Stempuzis   Architect

**Project Management**
*Consultant*
1950 Gough #404
San Francisco
CA 94109-3440
FAX 415.775.0326
VOX 415.775.0338
Programming
Architect Selection
Pre-Design
Design Management
Administration

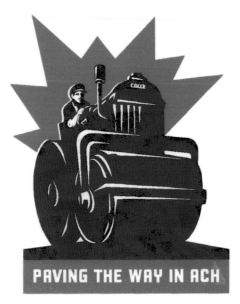

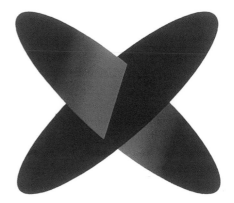

DESIGN FIRM | WEBSTER DESIGN ASSOCIATES
ART DIRECTOR | DAVE WEBSTER
DESIGNER/ILLUSTRATOR | ANDREY NAGORNY
CLIENT | ACH, INC.
TOOLS | MACROMEDIA FREEHAND

DESIGN FIRM | SHIMOKOCHI/REEVES
ART DIRECTORS | MAMORU SHIMOKOCHI, ANNE REEVES
DESIGNER | MAMORU SHIMOKOCHI
CLIENT | X-CENTURY STUDIOS
TOOLS | ADOBE ILLUSTRATOR

[internet:press]

DESIGN FIRM | LSL INDUSTRIES
DESIGNER | ELISABETH SPITALNY
CLIENT | JP DAVIS & COMPANY, INTERNET PRESS
TOOLS | ADOBE ILLUSTRATOR

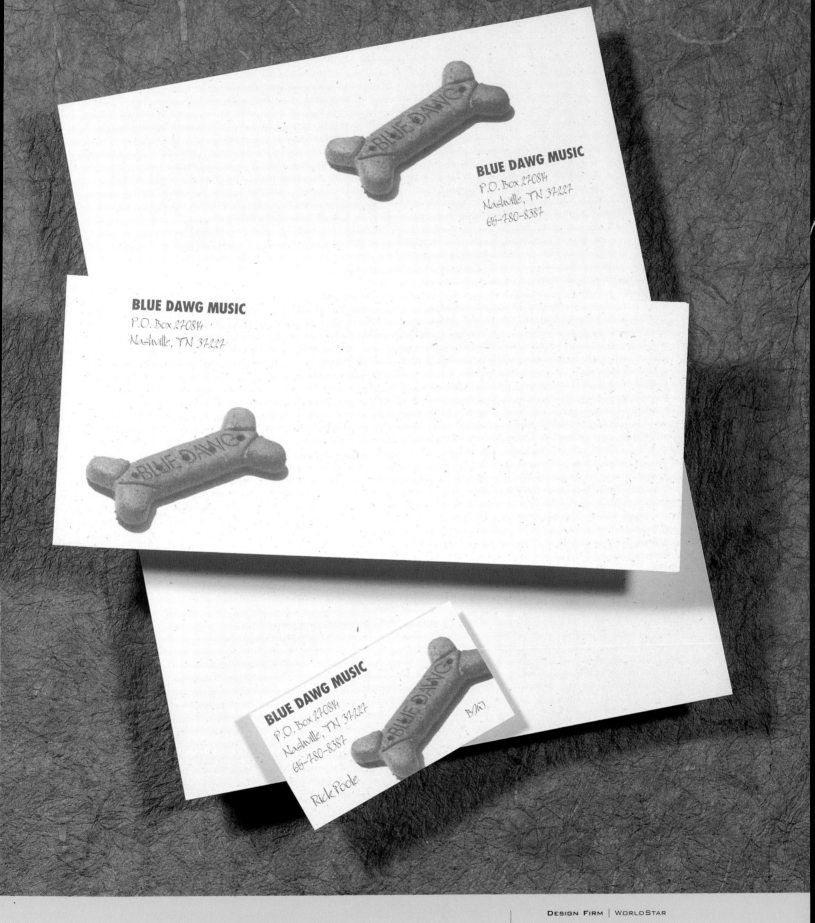

BLUE DAWG MUSIC
P.O. Box 270814
Nashville, TN 37227
615-780-8387

BLUE DAWG MUSIC
P.O. Box 270814
Nashville, TN 37227

BLUE DAWG MUSIC
P.O. Box 270814
Nashville, TN 37227
615-780-8387

Rick Poole

DESIGN FIRM | WORLDSTAR
ALL DESIGN | GREG GUHL
CLIENT | BLUE DAWG MUSIC
TOOLS | ADOBE PHOTOSHOP, ADOBE ILLUSTRATOR

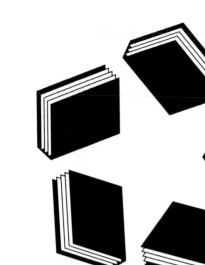

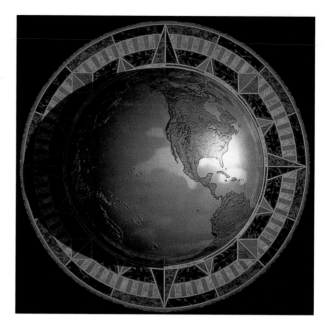

DESIGN FIRM | SULLIVAN PERKINS
ALL DESIGN | BRETT BARIDON
CLIENT | DALLAS PUBLIC LIBRARY

DESIGN FIRM | DESIGN GROUP WEST
ART DIRECTOR | JOAN MALONEY
ILLUSTRATOR | TRACY SABIN
CLIENT | HAHN/TRIZEC
TOOLS | STRATA STUDIO PRO

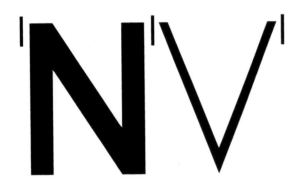

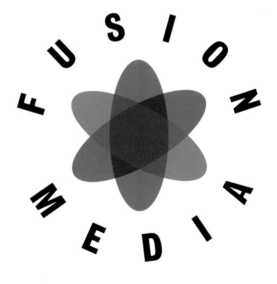

DESIGN FIRM | TANGRAM STRATEGIC DESIGN
ART DIRECTOR/DESIGNER/CREATIVE DIRECTOR | ENRICO SEMPI
CLIENT | ORDINE DEGLI ARCHITETTI DI NOVARA

DESIGN FIRM | MIRES DESIGN
ART DIRECTOR | JOHN BALL
DESIGNERS | JOHN BALL, DEBORAH HORN
CLIENT | FUSION MEDIA

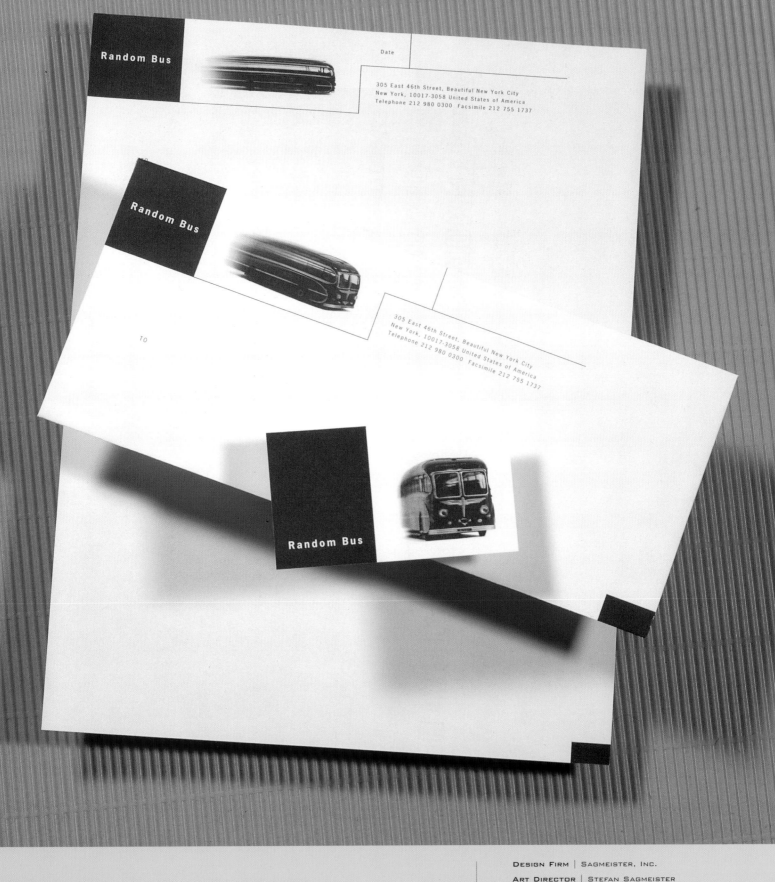

DESIGN FIRM | SAGMEISTER, INC.

ART DIRECTOR | STEFAN SAGMEISTER

DESIGNER | ERIC ZIM

PHOTOGRAPHY | TOM SCHIERLITZ

CLIENT | RANDOM BUS

TOOLS | MACINTOSH, 4 X 5 CAMERA

PAPER/PRINTING | STRATHMORE WRITING 25% COTTON

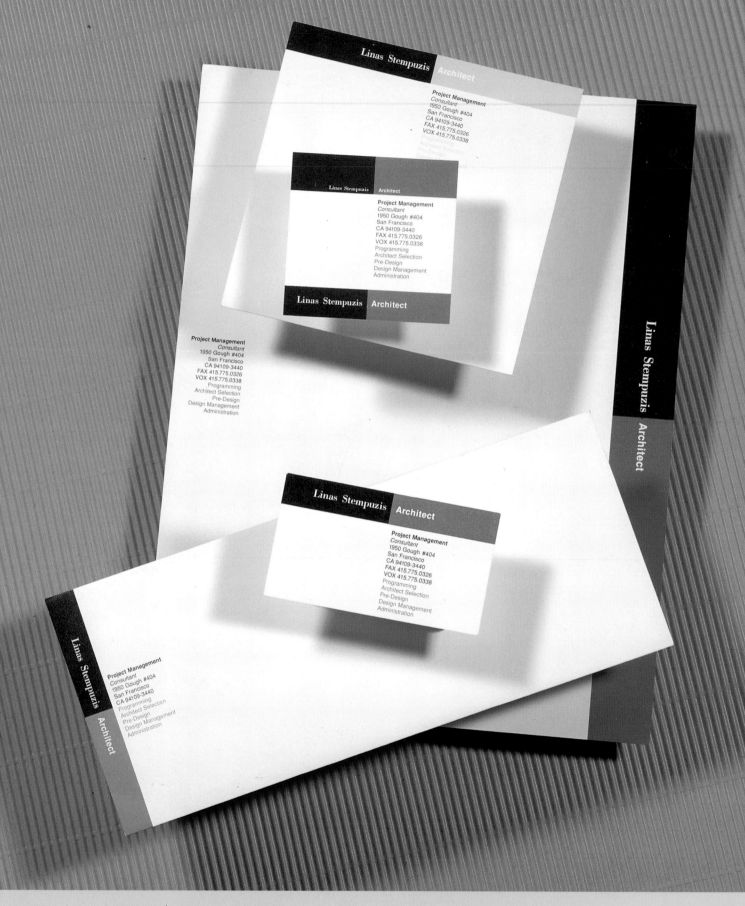

DESIGN FIRM | MELISSA PASSEHL DESIGN

ART DIRECTOR | MELISSA PASSEHL

DESIGNERS | MELISSA PASSEHL, JILL STEINFELD

CLIENT | LINAS STEMPUZIS

DESIGN FIRM | IMAGINE THAT, INC.

ALL DESIGN | SUE MANIAN

CLIENT | JIM MCGOWAN, AIA

TOOLS | MACROMEDIA FREEHAND

PAPER/PRINTING | CLASSIC CREST/CLARKS LITHO

DESIGN FIRM | SHIMOKOCHI/REEVES
ART DIRECTORS | MAMORU SHIMOKOCHI, ANNE REEVES
DESIGNER | MAMORU SHIMOKOCHI
CLIENT | IZEN
TOOLS | ADOBE ILLUSTRATOR
PAPER/PRINTING | GRAPHIKA LINEAL

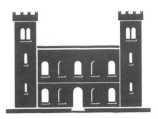

# CENTRO INTERCULTURALE
# TAVOLINO ROVESCIATO

DESIGN FIRM | TANGRAM STRATEGIC DESIGN
ART DIRECTOR/DESIGNER/CREATIVE DIRECTOR | ENRICO SEMPI
CLIENT | COMPACT
TOOLS | POWER MACINTOSH

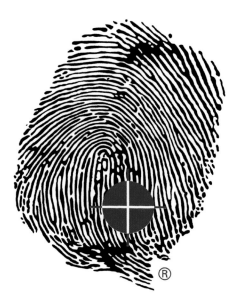

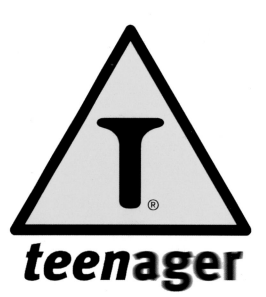

DESIGN FIRM | CATO BERRO DISEÑO
ALL DESIGN | GONZALO BERRO
CLIENT | CRESTA MAGNA/ENTERTAINMENT
TOOLS | ADOBE ILLUSTRATOR

ALL DESIGN | JOSÉ TORRES
CLIENT | TEENAGER BOUTIQUE
TOOLS | ADOBE PHOTOSHOP, MACROMEDIA FREEHAND

DESIGN FIRM | Rick Eiber Design (RED)

ART DIRECTOR/DESIGNER | Rick Eiber

ILLUSTRATORS | Dave D. Weller (logo), Gary Volk (hands)

CLIENT | On The Wall

PAPER/PRINTING | Speckletone two color (one metallic)
     over one color

Design, Construction & Maintenance of Fine Turf Surfaces ~ 19 Dermot Street South Oakleigh 3167  PH 9570 1809  FAX 9570 1809

DESIGN FIRM | WATTS GRAPHIC DESIGN
ART DIRECTORS/DESIGNERS | HELEN WATTS,
    PETER WATTS
CLIENT | GREEN CONCEPTS
TOOLS | MACINTOSH
PAPER/PRINTING | THREE COLOR

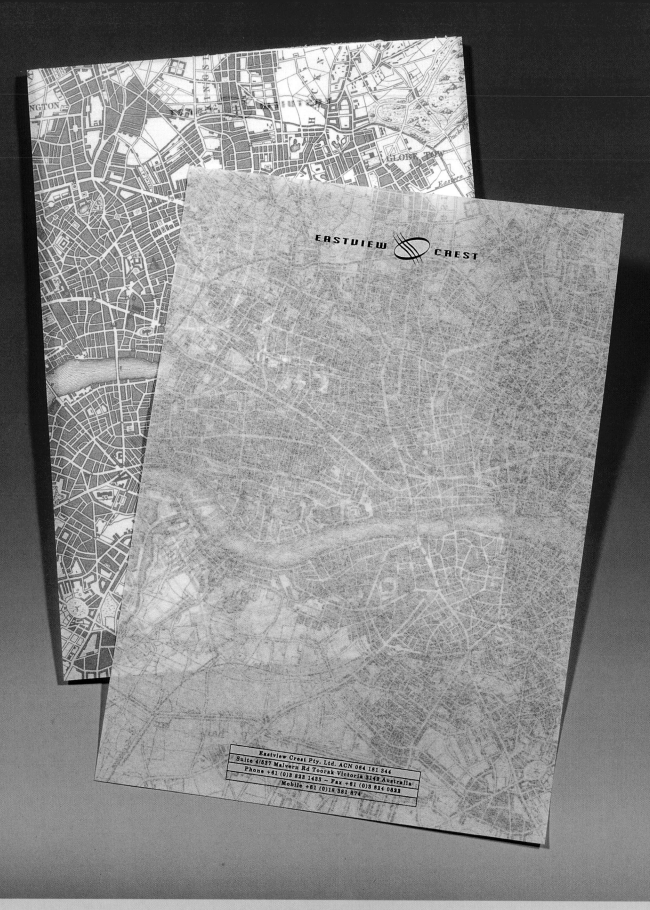

EASTVIEW CREST

Eastview Crest Pty. Ltd. ACN 064 181 344
Suite 4/537 Malvern Rd Toorak Victoria 3142 Australia
Phone +61 (0)3 823 1433 ~ Fax +61 (0)3 824 0822
Mobile +61 (0)18 381 874

DESIGN FIRM | WATTS GRAPHIC DESIGN

ART DIRECTORS/DESIGNERS | HELEN WATTS, PETER WATTS

CLIENT | EASTVIEW CREST

TOOLS | MACINTOSH

PAPER/PRINTING | PARCHMENT/ONE SIDE ONE COLOR,
ONE SIDE TWO COLOR

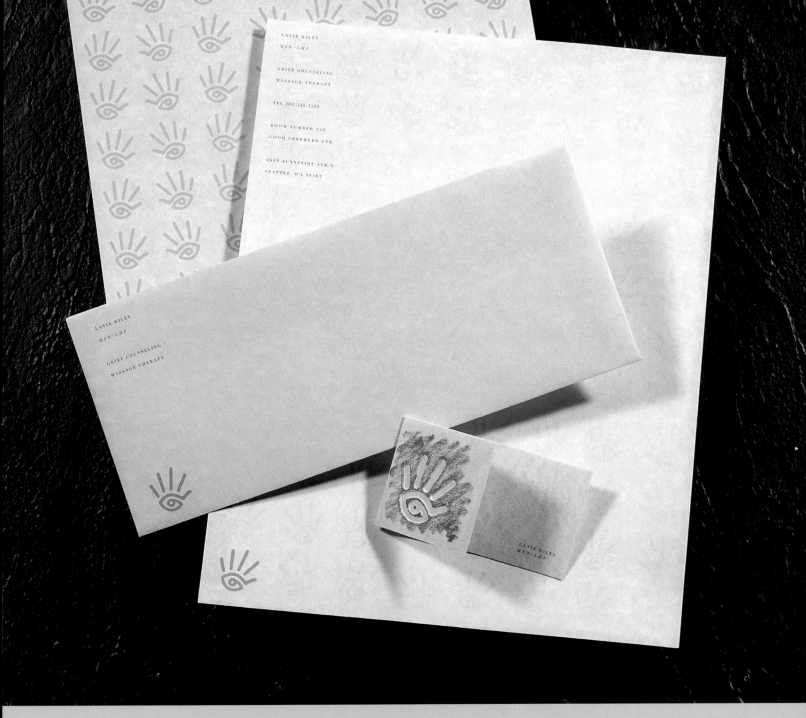

DESIGN FIRM | RICK EIBER DESIGN (RED)
ART DIRECTOR/DESIGNER | RICK EIBER
CLIENT | LANIE RILEY
PAPER/PRINTING | PARCHTONE

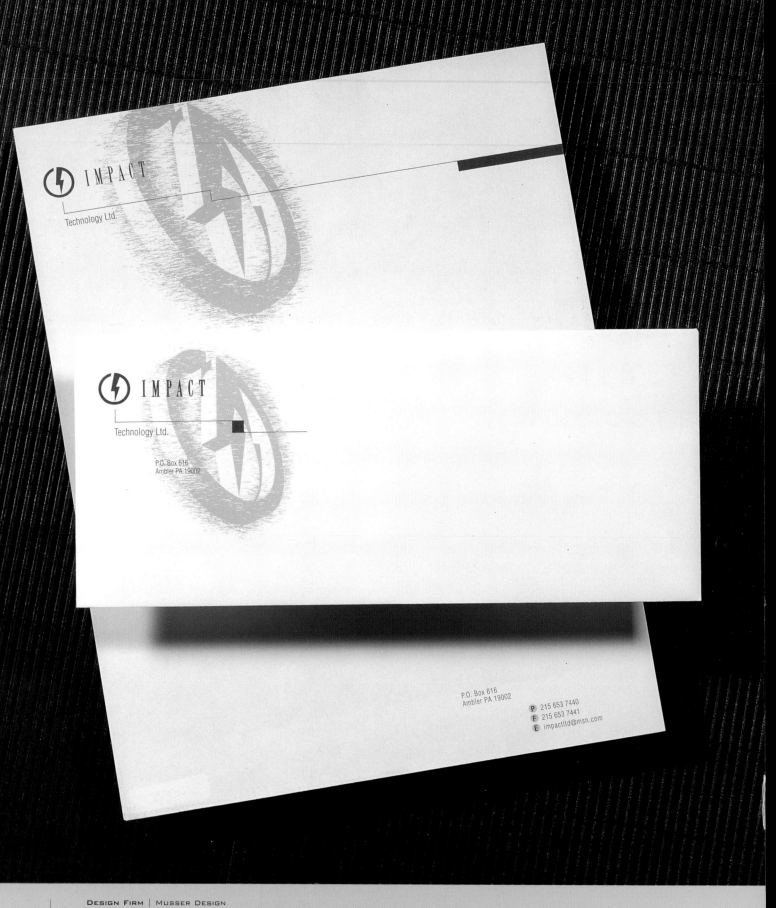

DESIGN FIRM | MUSSER DESIGN

ART DIRECTOR/DESIGNER | JERRY KING MUSSER

CLIENT | E W AND A

TOOLS | MACINTOSH QUADRA, ADOBE ILLUSTRATOR

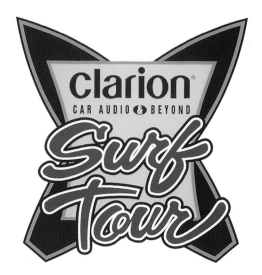

DESIGN FIRM | GILLIS & SMILER
ART DIRECTOR/DESIGNER | CHERYL GILLIS
CLIENT | CLARION SURF TOUR
TOOLS | ADOBE ILLUSTRATOR

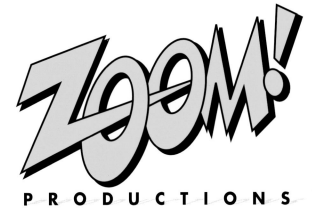

DESIGN FIRM | PENCIL NECK PRODUCTIONS
ART DIRECTOR | GARY HAWTHORNE
CLIENT | ZOOM! PRODUCTIONS
TOOLS | ADOBE ILLUSTRATOR

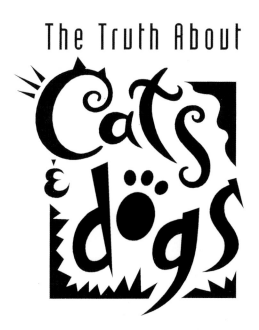

DESIGN FIRM | GILLIS & SMILER
ART DIRECTOR/DESIGNER | CHERYL GILLIS
CLIENT | NEW LINE CINEMA
TOOLS | ADOBE ILLUSTRATOR

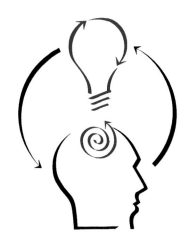

DESIGN FIRM | ROBERT BAILEY INCORPORATED
ALL DESIGN | CONNIE LIGHTNER
CLIENT | IDEA CATALYSTS, INC.
TOOLS | ADOBE ILLUSTRATOR

270 Lafayette Street Suite 904 New York NY 10012
Telephone 212 431 6745 Facsimile 212 431 6583

NAKED MUSIC NYC

Naked Music NYC    270 Lafayette Street  Suite 904  New York New York  10012  United States of America                    NAKED MUSIC NYC

NAKED MUSIC NYC

Jay Denes
T. 212 431 6745  F. 431 6583
270 Lafayette Street #904
New York NY 10012

DESIGN FIRM | SAGMEISTER, INC.

ART DIRECTOR | STEFAN SAGMEISTER

DESIGNERS | STEFAN SAGMEISTER, VERONICA OH

PHOTOGRAPHY | TOM SCHIERLITZ

CLIENT | NAKED MUSIC NYC

TOOLS | MACINTOSH, 4 X 5 CAMERA

PAPER/PRINTING | STRATHMORE WRITING 25% COTTON

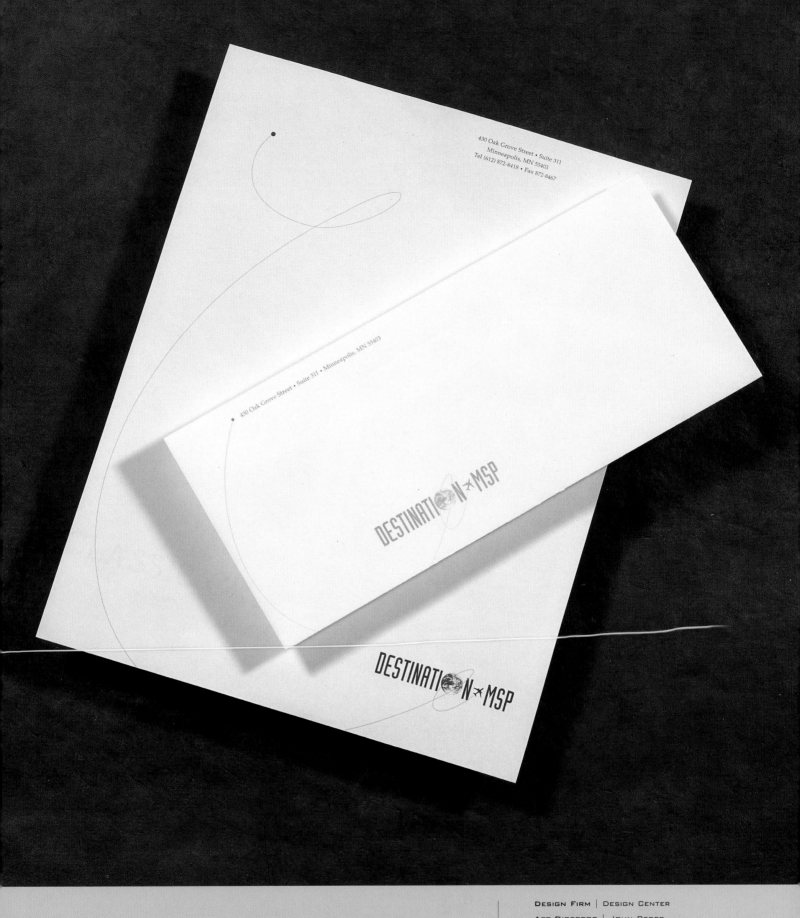

430 Oak Grove Street • Suite 311
Minneapolis, MN 55403
Tel (612) 872-8418 • Fax 872-8467

430 Oak Grove Street • Suite 311 • Minneapolis, MN 55403

DESTINATI☉N✈MSP

DESTINATI☉N✈MSP

DESIGN FIRM | DESIGN CENTER
ART DIRECTOR | JOHN REGER
DESIGNER | SHERWIN SWARTZROCK
CLIENT | DESTINATION MSP
TOOLS | MACINTOSH
PAPER/PRINTING | CLASSIC CREST/PRINTCRAFT

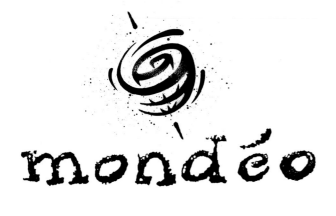

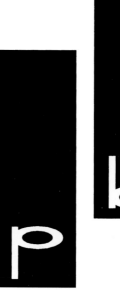

DESIGN FIRM | HORNALL ANDERSON DESIGN WORKS, INC.

ART DIRECTOR | JACK ANDERSON

DESIGNER | JACK ANDERSON, DAVID BATES

ILLUSTRATOR | DAVID BATES

CLIENT | CW GOURMET

DESIGN FIRM | XSNRG ILLUSTRATION AND DESIGN

ALL DESIGN | KEVIN BALL

CLIENT | 8 BALL MUSIC

TOOLS | CORELDRAW

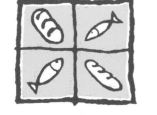

# LOAVES+FISHES

DESIGN FIRM | CREATIVE COMPANY

ALL DESIGN | RICK YURK

CLIENT | LOAVES & FISHES

TOOLS | MACINTOSH

DESIGN FIRM | A1 DESIGN

DESIGNER | AMY GREGG

CLIENT | PETER BELANGER PHOTOGRAPHY

TOOLS | MACINTOSH QUADRA, ADOBE ILLUSTRATOR

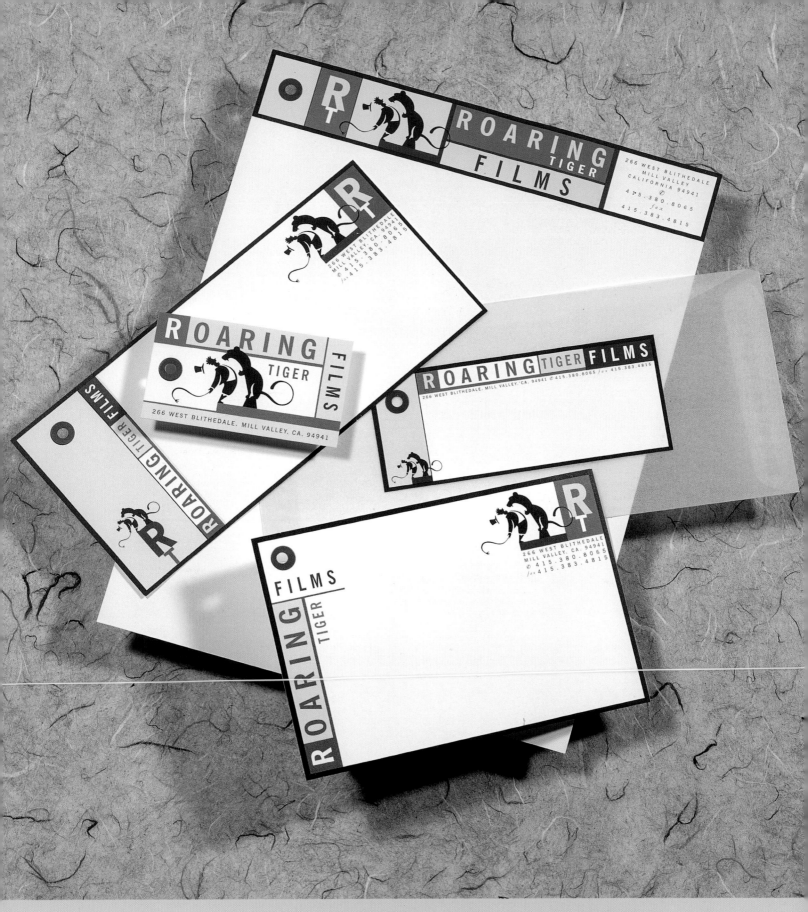

DESIGN FIRM | DOGSTAR
ART DIRECTOR | JENNIFER MARTIN
DESIGNER/ILLUSTRATOR | RODNEY DAVIDSON
CLIENT | ROARING TIGER FILMS
TOOLS | ADOBE ILLUSTRATOR, STREAMLINE,
MACROMEDIA FREEHAND

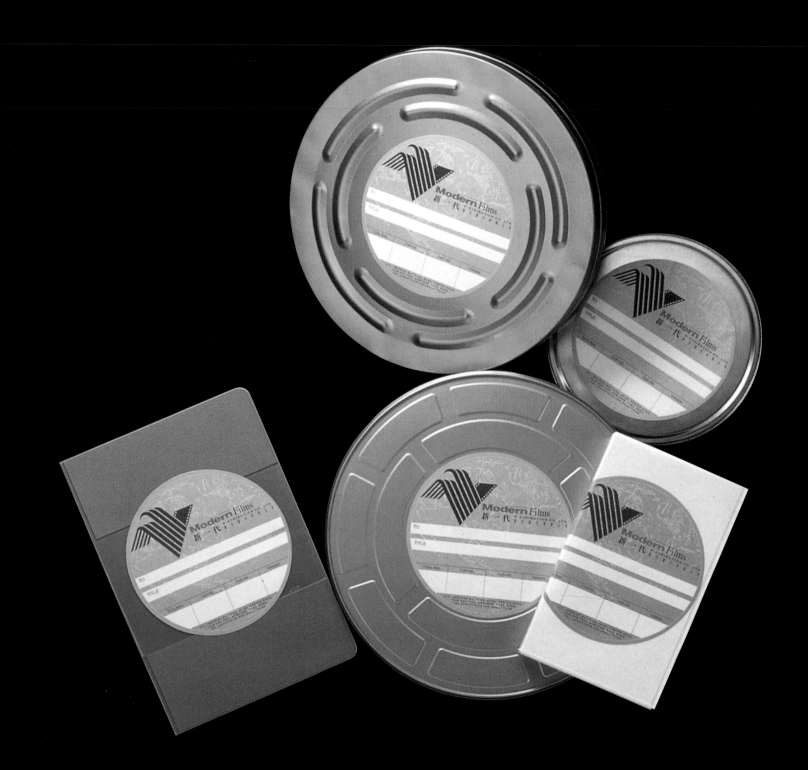

DESIGN FIRM | GRAND DESIGN COMPANY
ART DIRECTOR | GRAND SO
DESIGNER | GRAND SO, KWONG ETTI MAN
ILLUSTRATOR | KWONG ETTI MAN
CLIENT | MODERN FILMS

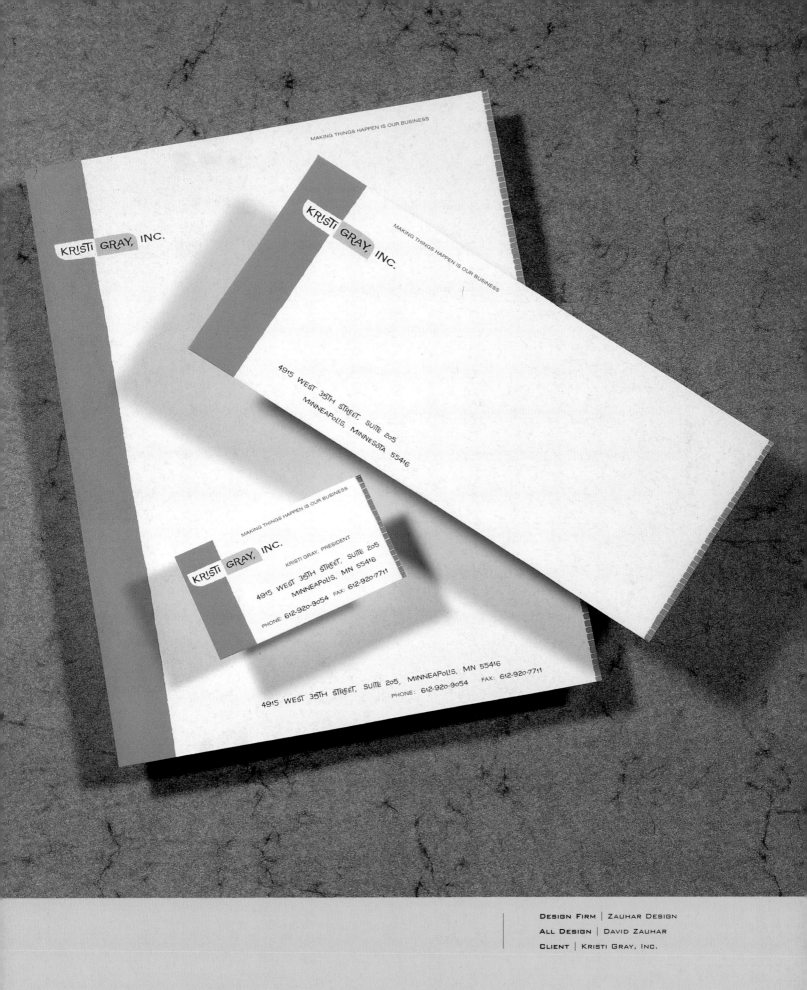

DESIGN FIRM | ZAUHAR DESIGN
ALL DESIGN | DAVID ZAUHAR
CLIENT | KRISTI GRAY, INC.

4016 Farm Hill Blvd #103
Redwood City, California
94061-1017

Amy Jo Kim
Creative Director

4016 Farm Hill Blvd #103
Redwood City, California
94061-1017

Tel 415.369.0313
Fax 415.369.0939

amyjo@naima.com
http://www.naima.com

Strategic Design for Online Environments

Amy Jo Kim
Creative Director

4016 Farm Hill Blvd #103
Redwood City, California
94061-1017

Tel 415.369.0313
Fax 415.369.0939

amyjo@naima.com
http://www.naima.com

Strategic Design for Online Environments

Strategic Design
for Online Environments

4016 Farm Hill Blvd #103
Redwood City, California
94061-1017

Tel 415.369.0313
Fax 415.369.0939

amyjo@naima.com
http://www.naima.com

DESIGN FIRM | AERIAL

ART DIRECTOR/DESIGNER | TRACY MOON

CLIENT | AMY JO KIM/NAIMA PRODUCTIONS

TOOLS | ADOBE PHOTOSHOP, QUARKXPRESS

PAPER/PRINTING | CLASSIC CREST SOLAR WHITE 80 LB.

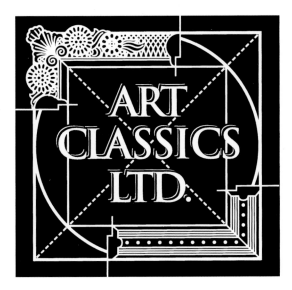

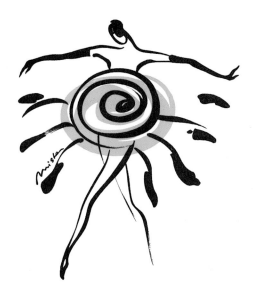

DESIGN FIRM | PHOENIX CREATIVE, ST. LOUIS
ALL DESIGN | ED MANTELS-SEEKER
CLIENT | ART CLASSICS LTD.
TOOLS | MACROMEDIA FREEHAND

DESIGN FIRM | MICHAEL STANARD DESIGN, INC.
ART DIRECTOR | MICHAEL STANARD
DESIGNER | KRISTY VANDEKERCKHOVE
CLIENT | JOHN MANCINI
TOOLS | MACINTOSH, ADOBE ILLUSTRATOR

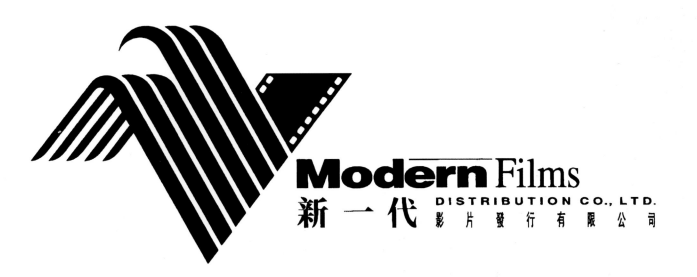

DESIGN FIRM | GRAND DESIGN COMPANY
ART DIRECTOR | GRAND SO
DESIGNER | GRAND SO, KWONG ETTI MAN
ILLUSTRATOR | KWONG ETTI MAN
CLIENT | MODERN FILMS

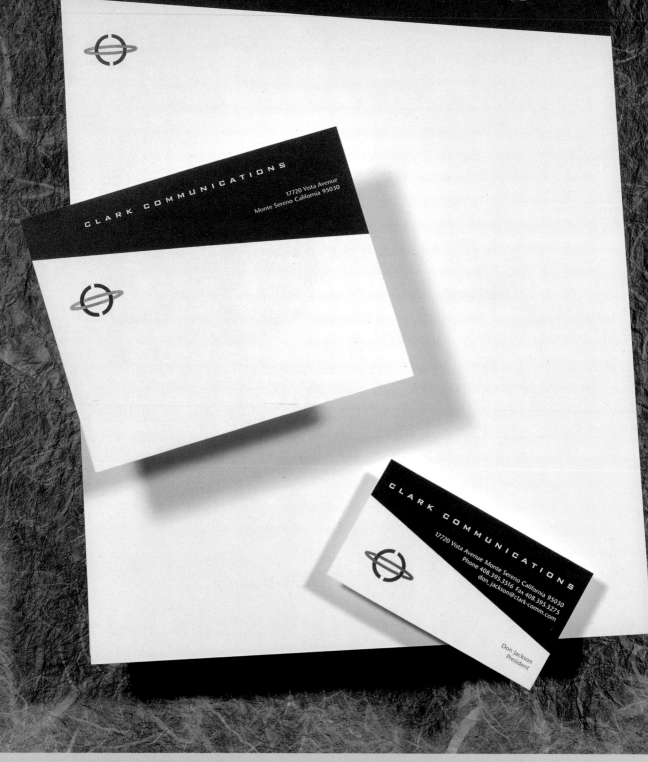

CLARK COMMUNICATIONS

17720 Vista Avenue Monte Sereno California 95030
Phone 408.395.3516 Fax 408.395.3275
don_jackson@clark-comm.com

CLARK COMMUNICATIONS

17720 Vista Avenue
Monte Sereno California 95030

CLARK COMMUNICATIONS

17720 Vista Avenue Monte Sereno California 95030
Phone 408.395.3516 Fax 408.395.3275
don_jackson@clark-comm.com

Don Jackson
President

**DESIGN FIRM** | MELISSA PASSEHL DESIGN
**ART DIRECTOR/DESIGNER** | MELISSA PASSEHL
**CLIENT** | CLARK COMMUNICATIONS

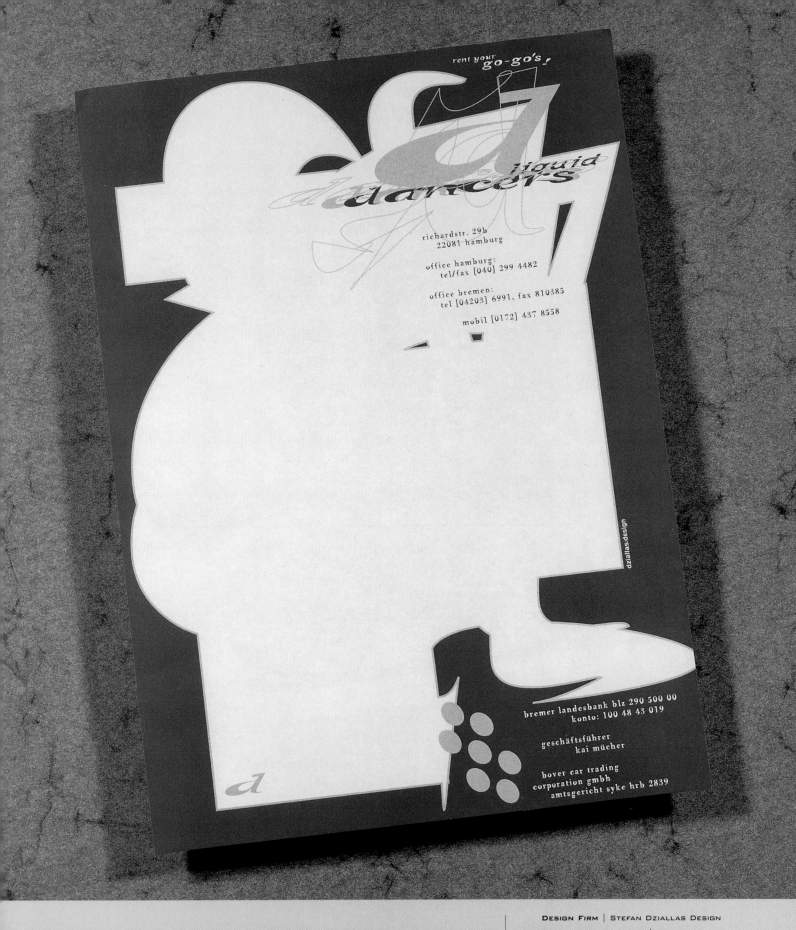

**Design Firm** | Stefan Dziallas Design

**Designer/Illustrator** | Stefan Dziallas

**Client** | Stefan Dziallas

**Tools** | Adobe Illustrator, QuarkXPress,
Macintosh

# ~ALCAROTTi
## CENTRO SPORTIVO

DESIGN FIRM | TANGRAM STRATEGIC DESIGN
ART DIRECTOR/DESIGNER | ANTONELLA TREVISAN
CLIENT | CENTRO SPORTIVO ALCAROTTI
TOOLS | POWER MACINTOSH

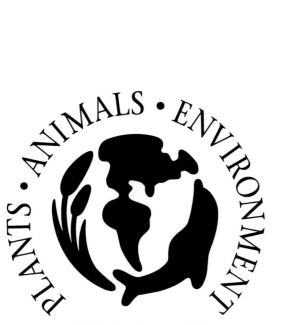

DESIGN FIRM | GET SMART DESIGN COMPANY
ART DIRECTOR | JEFF MACFARLANE
DESIGNER/ILLUSTRATOR | TOM CULBERTSON
CLIENT | WCB/MCGRAW-HILL PUBLISHERS
TOOLS | MACROMEDIA FREEHAND

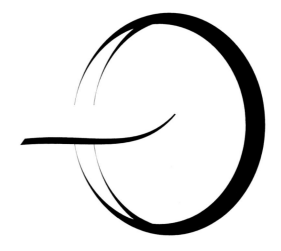

DESIGN FIRM | EYE DESIGN INCORPORATED
ALL DESIGN | ROBIN MEYERS
CLIENT | DYNAMIC DECISIONS/PEI-O
TOOLS | ADOBE ILLUSTRATOR
PAPER/PRINTING | PMS 485

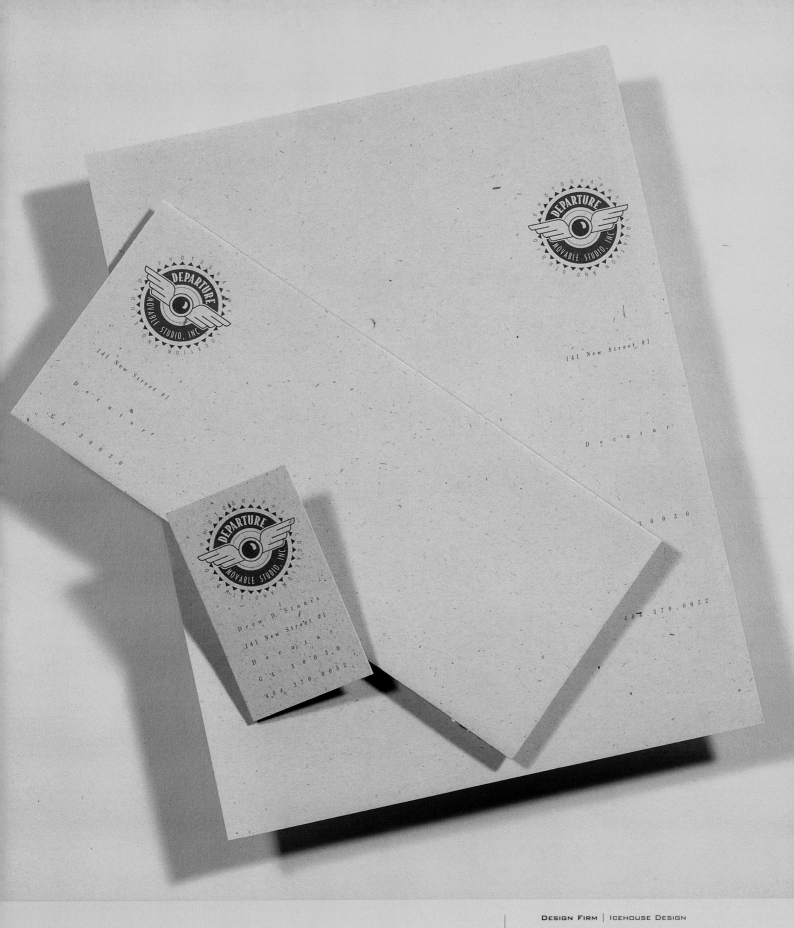

DESIGN FIRM | ICEHOUSE DESIGN

ART DIRECTOR | PATTIE BELLE HASTINGS

DESIGNER/ILLUSTRATOR | BJORN AKSELSEN

CLIENT | DEPARTURE

TOOLS | POWER MACINTOSH

PAPER/PRINTING | FRENCH SPECKLETONE

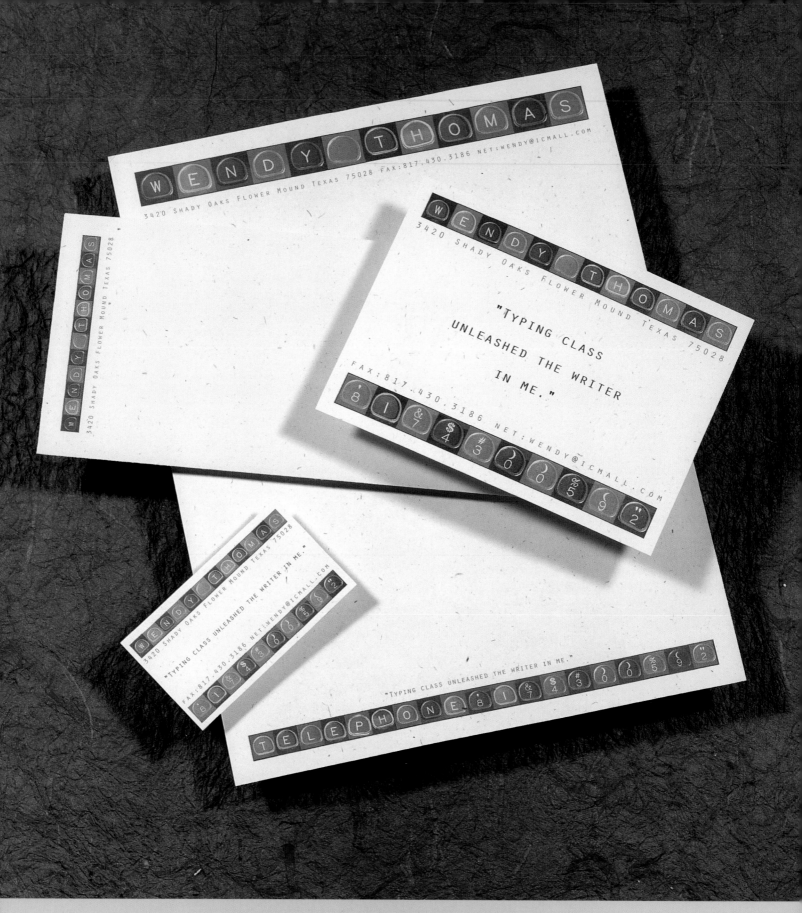

DESIGN FIRM | ELENA DESIGN

ART DIRECTOR/DESIGNER | ELENA BACA

ILLUSTRATOR | PHOTOTONE ALPHABETS

CLIENT | WENDY THOMAS

TOOLS | QUARKXPRESS

PAPER/PRINTING | FRENCH SPECKELTONE

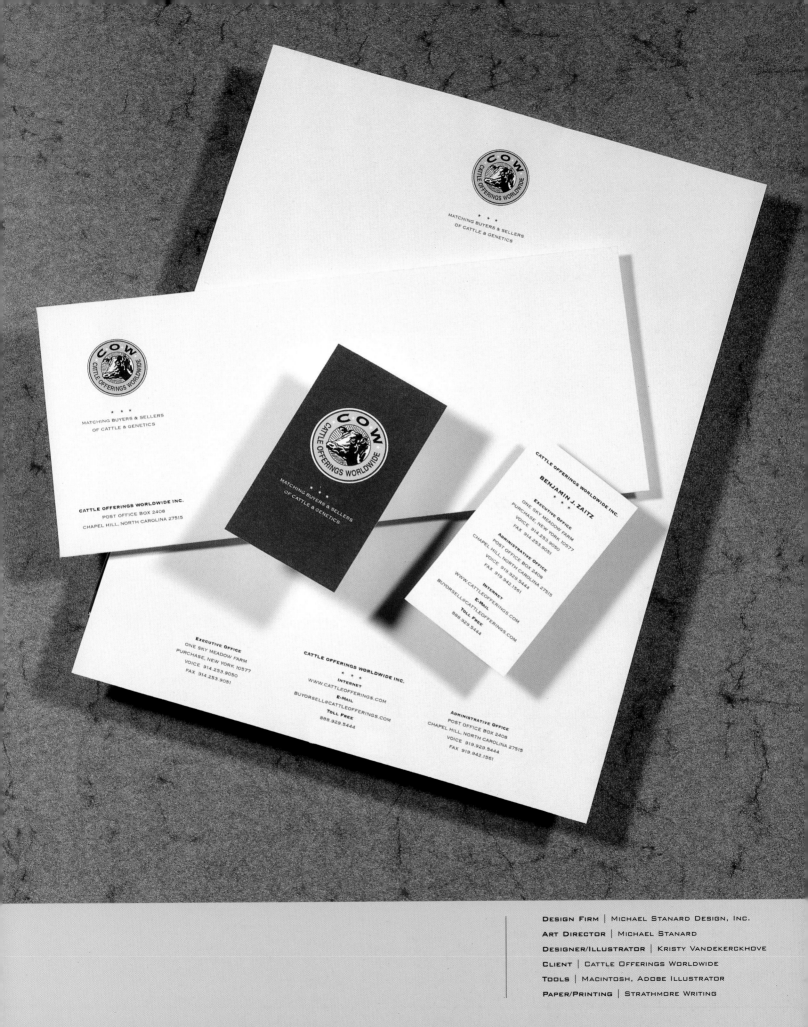

DESIGN FIRM | MICHAEL STANARD DESIGN, INC.

ART DIRECTOR | MICHAEL STANARD

DESIGNER/ILLUSTRATOR | KRISTY VANDEKERCKHOVE

CLIENT | CATTLE OFFERINGS WORLDWIDE

TOOLS | MACINTOSH, ADOBE ILLUSTRATOR

PAPER/PRINTING | STRATHMORE WRITING

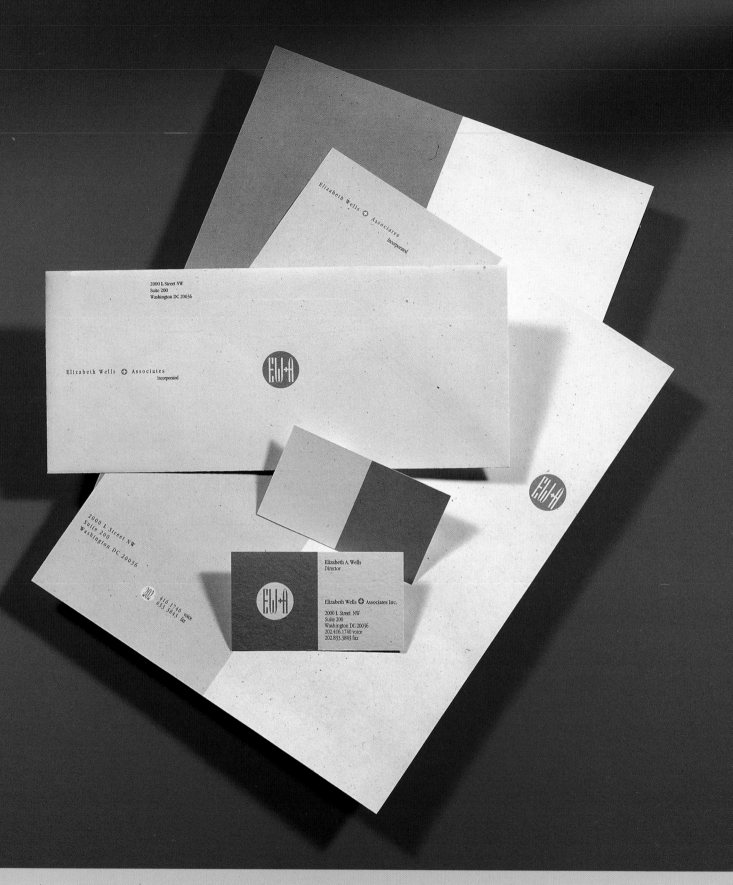

DESIGN FIRM | ANDERSON-THOMAS DESIGN, INC.

ART DIRECTOR/DESIGNER | JOEL ANDERSON

CLIENT | STAR SONG COMMUNICATIONS

TOOLS | QUARKXPRESS, ADOBE ILLUSTRATOR

PAPER/PRINTING | CLASSIC CREST/BLACK PLUS ONE PMS

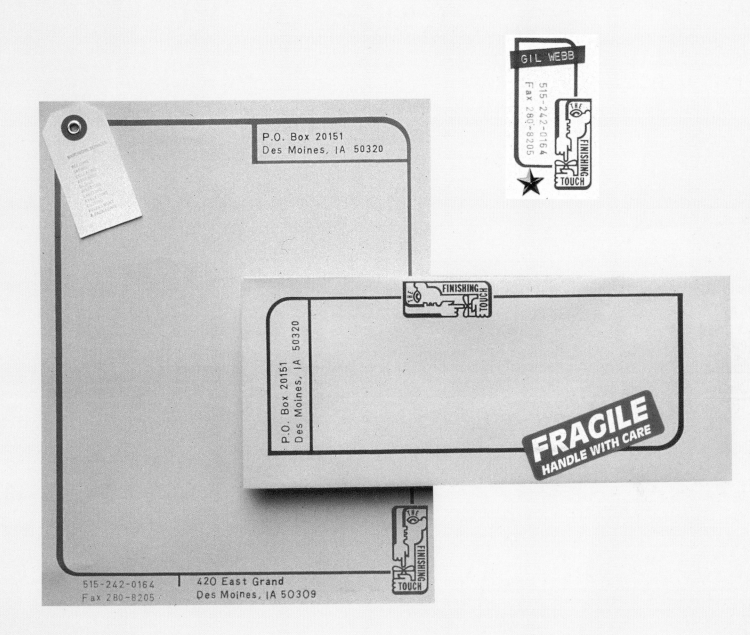

DESIGN FIRM | SAYLES GRAPHIC DESIGN

ALL DESIGN | JOHN SAYLES

CLIENT | THE FINISHING TOUCH

PAPER/PRINTING | INCENTIVE 100 LB. AND

MANILA TAG/ OFFSET AND RUBBER STAMP

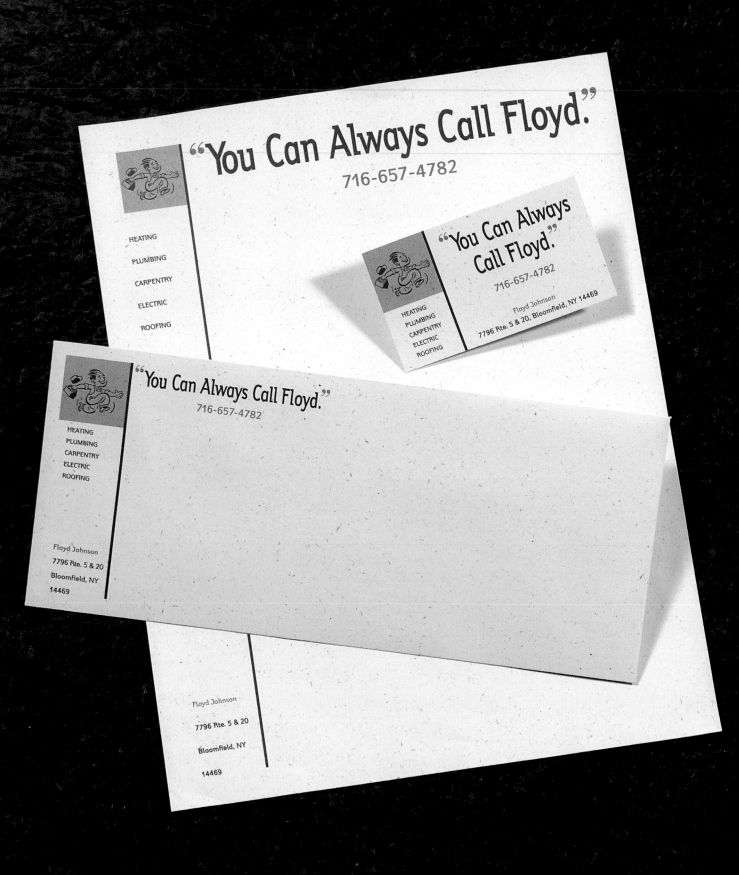

DESIGN FIRM | LYNN WOOD DESIGN
ART DIRECTOR/DESIGNER | LYNN WOOD
ILLUSTRATOR | MODIFIED CLIP ART
CLIENT | FLOYD JOHNSON
TOOLS | QUARKXPRESS, ADOBE ILLUSTRATOR, POWER MACINTOSH
PAPER/PRINTING | BENEFIT/GRAPHIC BROKERAGE

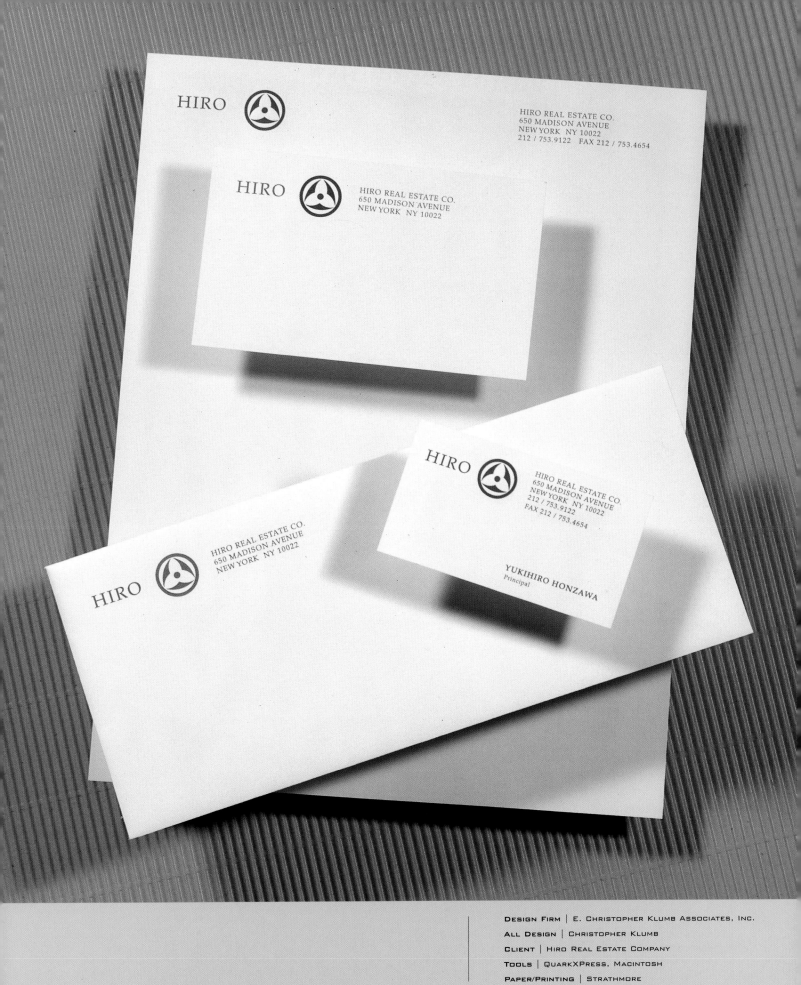

DESIGN FIRM │ E. CHRISTOPHER KLUMB ASSOCIATES, INC.

ALL DESIGN │ CHRISTOPHER KLUMB

CLIENT │ HIRO REAL ESTATE COMPANY

TOOLS │ QUARKXPRESS, MACINTOSH

PAPER/PRINTING │ STRATHMORE

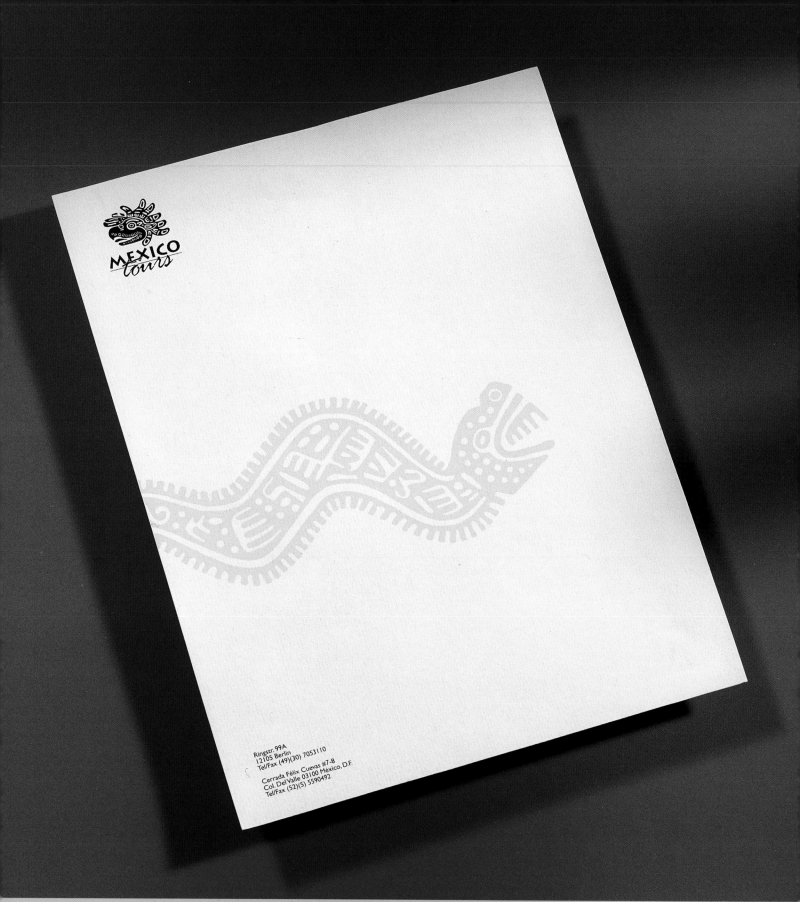

Ringstr. 99A
12105 Berlin
Tel/Fax (49)(30) 7053110

Cerrada Félix Cuevas #7-8
Col. Del Valle 03100 México, D.F.
Tel/Fax (52)(5) 5590492

DESIGN FIRM | ZAPPATA DESIGNERS

ART DIRECTOR/DESIGNER | IBO ANGULO

CLIENT | MEXICO TOURS (TOURIST AGENCY IN GERMANY)

TOOLS | MACROMEDIA FREEHAND

PAPER/PRINTING | RECYCLED/SILKSCREEN

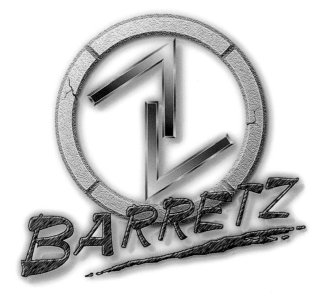

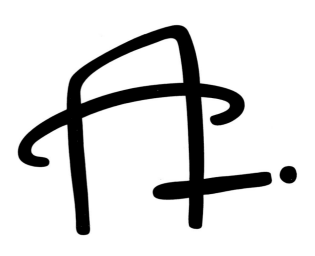

**DESIGN FIRM** | XSNRG ILLUSTRATION AND DESIGN
**ALL DESIGN** | KEVIN BALL
**CLIENT** | BARRETZ
**TOOLS** | CORELDRAW, PICTURE PUBLISHER

**DESIGN FIRM** | DOGSTAR
**ART DIRECTOR** | MARTIN LEEDS/CIGAR AFICIONADO
**DESIGNER/ILLUSTRATOR** | RODNEY DAVIDSON
**CLIENT** | CIGAR AFICIONADO
**TOOLS** | ADOBE ILLUSTRATOR, STREAMLINE, MACROMEDIA FREEHAND

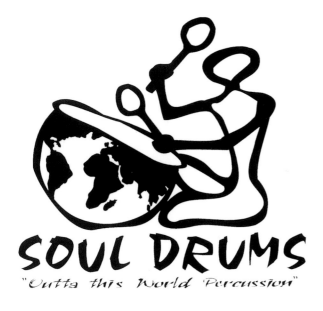

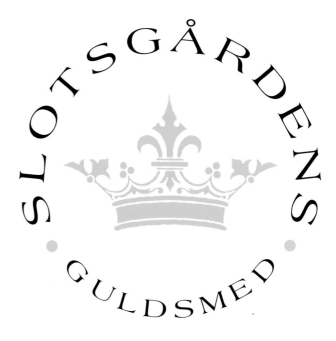

**DESIGN FIRM** | XSNRG ILLUSTRATION AND DESIGN
**ALL DESIGN** | KEVIN BALL
**CLIENT** | SOUL DRUMS
**TOOLS** | CORELDRAW

**ART DIRECTOR/DESIGNER** | ATHENA WINDELEV
**CLIENT** | SLOTSGÅRDENS GULDSMED, GOLDSMITH

PINNACLE ALLIANCE
*Achieving Excellence Through
Global Teamwork*

JPMorgan

CSC

ANDERSEN
CONSULTING

AT&T

© Bell Atlantic

PINNACLE ALLIANCE
*Achieving Excellence Through
Global Teamwork*

DESIGN FIRM | RAMONA HUTKO DESIGN

ART DIRECTOR/DESIGNER | RAMONA HUTKO

PHOTOGRAPHER | SHAWN HUTKO

CLIENT | PINNACLE ALLIANCE

TOOLS | ADOBE PHOTOSHOP, QUARKXPRESS

PAPER/PRINTING | MOHAWK SUPERFINE WHITE ESS SHELL

FINISH 80 LB. TEXT

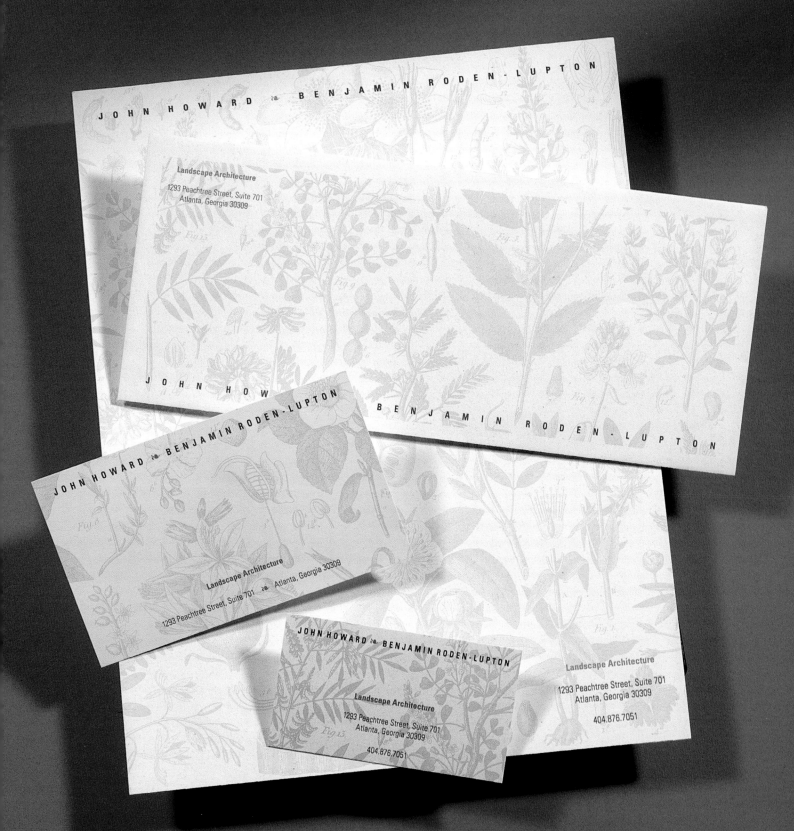

DESIGN FIRM | ICEHOUSE DESIGN
ART DIRECTOR/DESIGNER | PATTIE BELLE HASTINGS
CLIENT | JOHN HOWARD/BENJAMIN RODEN-LUPTON
TOOLS | POWER MACINTOSH
PAPER/PRINTING | CLASSIC CREST

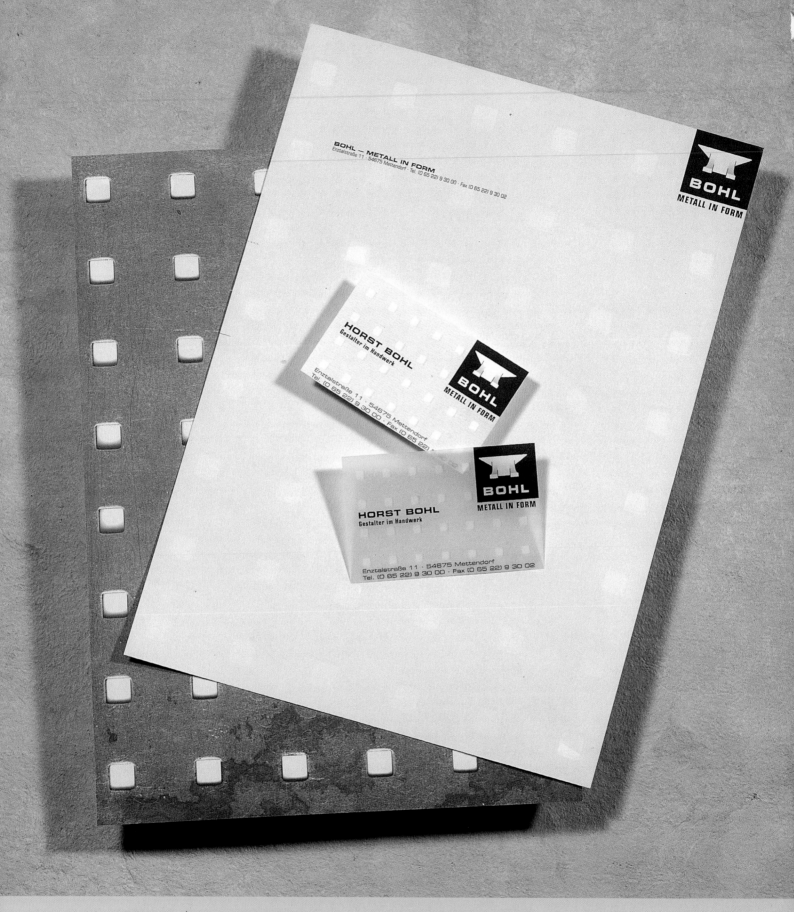

DESIGN FIRM | BOHL
ART DIRECTOR | STEFAN BOHL
CLIENT | BOHL METALL IN FORM
TOOLS | MACINTOSH

DESIGN FIRM | JOHN GAMBELL GRAPHIC DESIGN LLC

ART DIRECTOR | JOHN GAMBELL

DESIGNERS | JOHN GAMBELL, CHARLES ROUTHIER

CLIENT | ALBIS TURLINGTON ARCHITECTS LLC

TOOLS | QUARKXPRESS, ADOBE ILLUSTRATOR

PAPER/PRINTING | CRANES CREST 28 LB. FLOUR
WHITE/LEHAMN BROTHERS, INC., NEW HAVEN

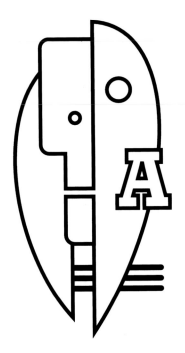

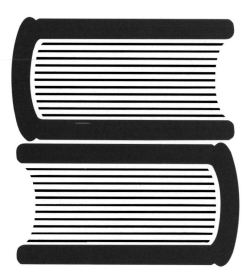

DESIGN FIRM | VOSS DESIGN
ALL DESIGN | AXEL VOSS
CLIENT | ART 'N STUFF

DESIGN FIRM | JEFF FISHER LOGOMOTIVES
ALL DESIGN | JEFF FISHER
CLIENT | SHLEIFER MARKETING COMMUNICATIONS, AGENCY FOR
SAMUELS YOELIN KANTOR SEYMOUR AND SPINRAD
TOOLS | MACROMEDIA FREEHAND

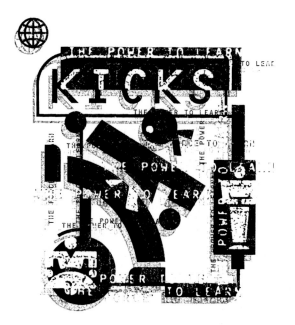

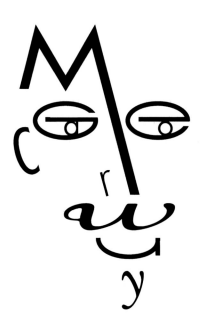

DESIGN FIRM | INSIGHT DESIGN COMMUNICATIONS
ALL DESIGNS | SHERRIE AND TRACY HOLDEMAN
CLIENT | KICKS
TOOLS | POWER MACINTOSH, MACROMEDIA FREEHAND,
ADOBE PHOTOSHOP

DESIGN FIRM | COMMONWEALTH CREATIVE ASSOCIATES
ART DIRECTOR/DESIGNER | ADAM RUDIKOFF
CLIENT | MCGOWAN EYECARE
TOOLS | MACINTOSH

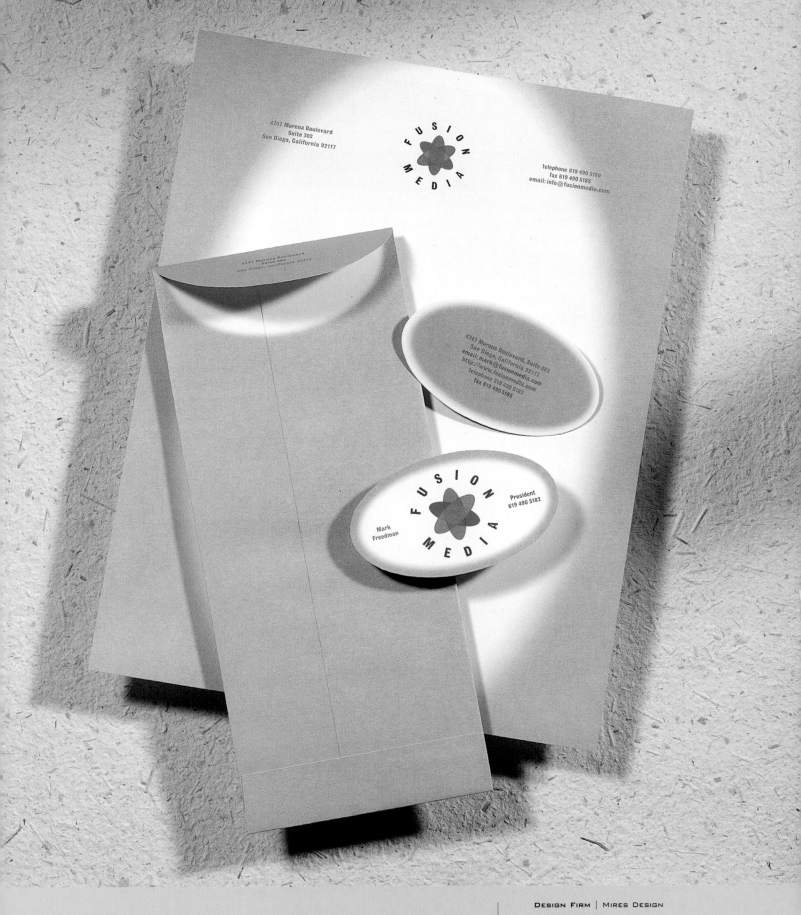

DESIGN FIRM │ MIRES DESIGN

ART DIRECTOR │ JOHN BALL

DESIGNERS │ JOHN BALL, DOBORAH HORN

CLIENT │ FUSION MEDIA

PAPER/PRINTING │ STARWHITE

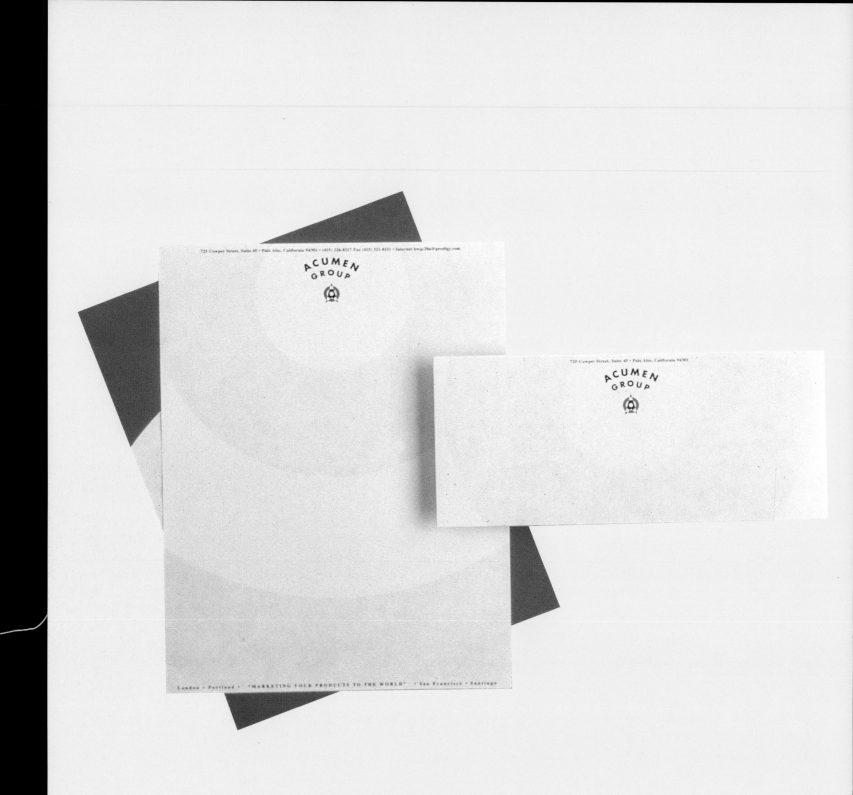

DESIGN FIRM | SAYLES GRAPHIC DESIGN

ALL DESIGN | JOHN SAYLES

CLIENT | ACUMEN GROUP

PAPER/PRINTING | GRAPHIKA WHITE PARCHMENT/OFFSET

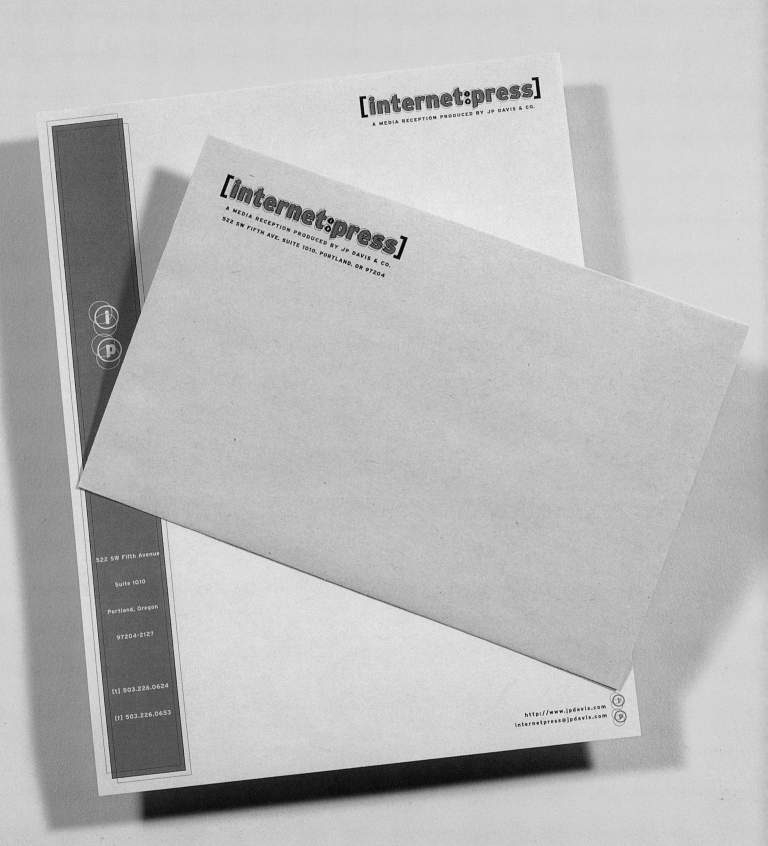

DESIGN FIRM | LSL INDUSTRIES
DESIGNER | ELISABETH SPITALNY
CLIENT | JP DAVIS & COMPANY, INTERNET PRESS
TOOLS | QUARKXPRESS, ADOBE ILLUSTRATOR
PAPER/PRINTING | FRENCH NEWSPRINT AGED/OFFSET

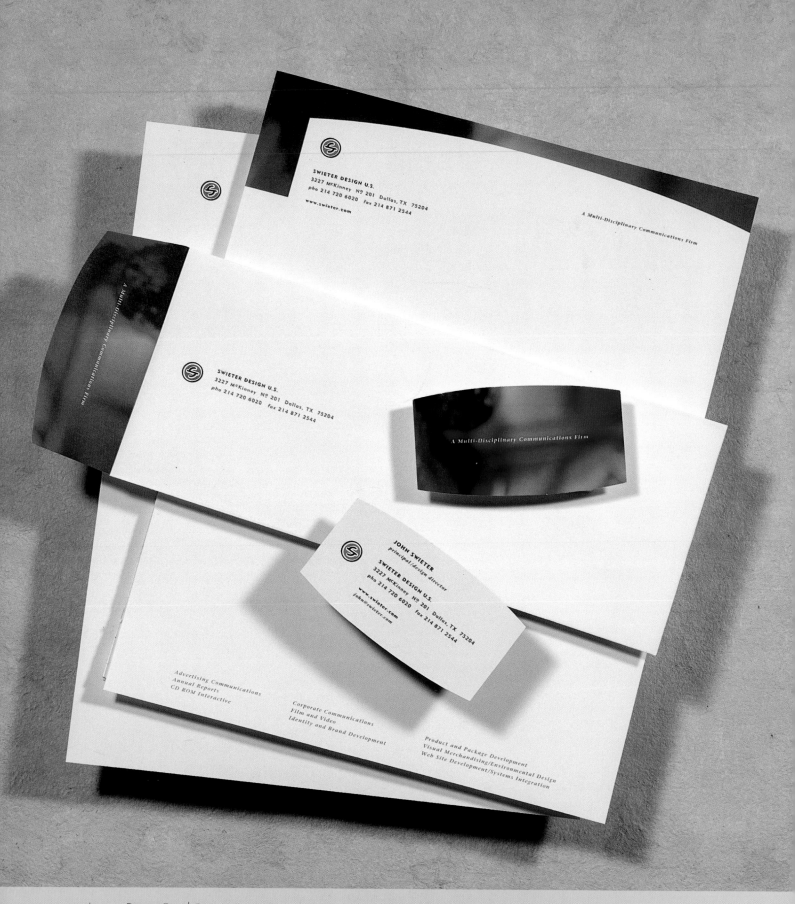

SWIETER DESIGN U.S.
3227 McKinney № 201 Dallas, TX 75204
pho 214 720 6020   fax 214 871 2544
www.swieter.com

A Multi-Disciplinary Communications Firm

SWIETER DESIGN U.S.
3227 McKinney № 201 Dallas, TX 75204
pho 214 720 6020   fax 214 871 2544

A Multi-Disciplinary Communications Firm

A Multi-Disciplinary Communications Firm

JOHN SWIETER
principal/design director
SWIETER DESIGN U.S.
3227 McKinney № 201 Dallas, TX 75204
pho 214 720 6020   fax 214 871 2544
www.swieter.com
john@swieter.com

Advertising Communications
Annual Reports
CD ROM Interactive

Corporate Communications
Film and Video
Identity and Brand Development

Product and Package Development
Visual Merchandising/Environmental Design
Web Site Development/Systems Integration

DESIGN FIRM | SWIETER DESIGN
ART DIRECTOR | JOHN SWIETER
DESIGNER | MARK FORD
CLIENT | SWIETER DESIGN
TOOLS | ADOBE PHOTOSHOP
PAPER/PRINTING | COATED/FOUR COLOR

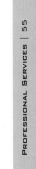

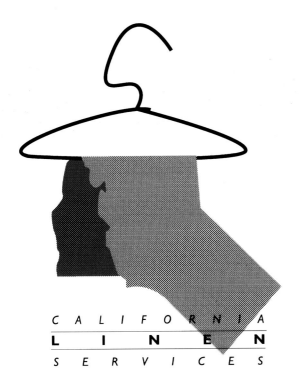

CALIFORNIA
L I N E N
S E R V I C E S

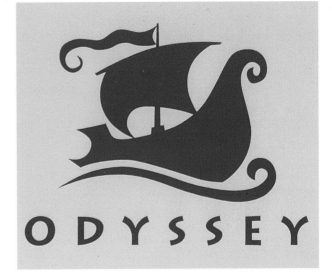

ODYSSEY

DESIGN FIRM | ADELE BASS + CO. DESIGN
ALL DESIGN | ADELE BASS
CLIENT | CALIFORNIA LINEN SERVICES
TOOLS | ADOBE ILLUSTRATOR

DESIGN FIRM | TRACY SABIN GRAPHIC DESIGN
ART DIRECTOR | ELISABETH PETERS
DESIGNER/ILLUSTRATOR | TRACY SABIN
CLIENT | HARCOURT BRACE & COMPANY/ODYSSEY
TOOLS | ADOBE ILLUSTRATOR

# C H A L M E R ⊕ H V E D E H A V E

DESIGN FIRM | TRANSPARENT OFFICE
ART DIRECTOR/DESIGNER | VIBEKE NØDSKOV
CLIENT | CHALMER + HVEDEHAVE
TOOLS | QUARKXPRESS, ADOBE ILLUSTRATOR

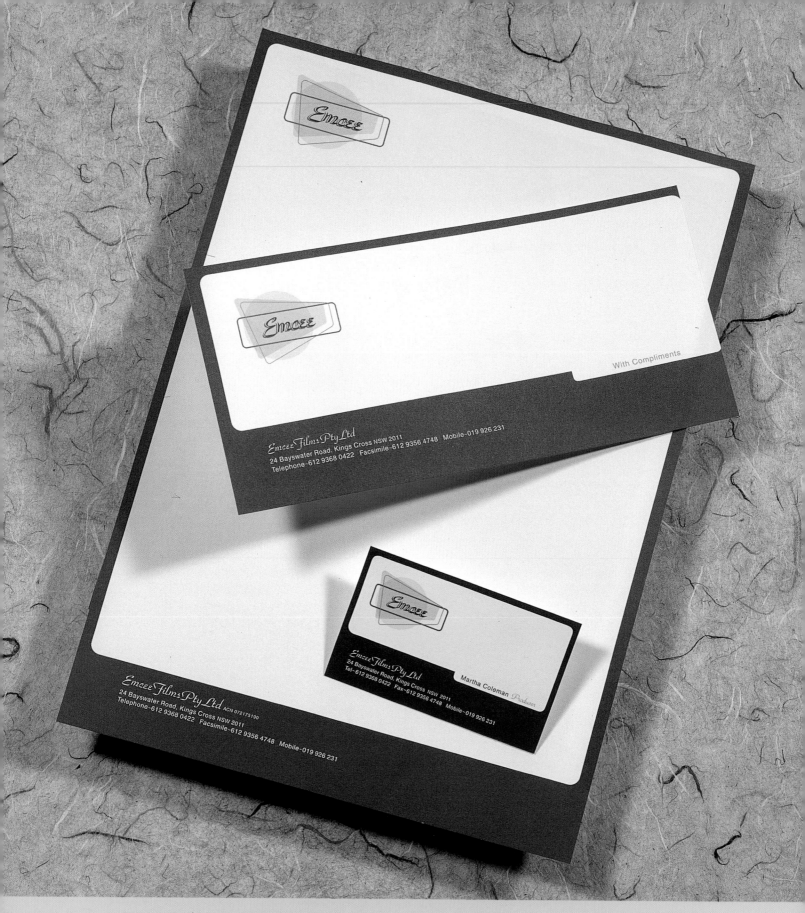

DESIGN FIRM | LUCY WALKER GRAPHIC DESIGN

ART DIRECTOR/DESIGNER | LUCY WALKER

CLIENT | EMCEE FILMS PTY. LTD.

TOOLS | ADOBE ILLUSTRATOR

PAPER/PRINTING | OCM IVORY WOVE

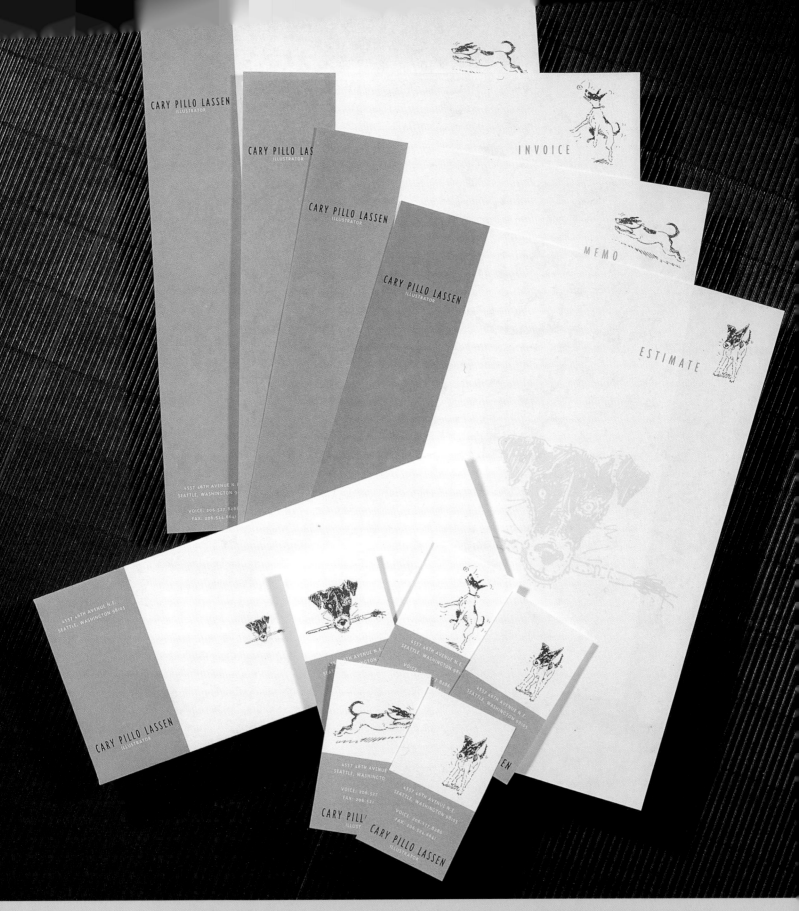

DESIGN FIRM | BELYEA DESIGN ALLIANCE
ART DIRECTOR | PATRICIA BELYEA
DESIGNER | TIM RUSZEL
ILLUSTRATOR | CARY PILLO LASSEN
CLIENT | CARY PILLO LASSEN

DESIGN FIRM | TANAGRAM

DESIGNER/ILLUSTRATOR | ANTHONY MA

CLIENT | LANKMAR CORPORATION

TOOLS | MACROMEDIA FREEHAND, ADOBE PHOTOSHOP

DESIGN FIRM | GILLIS & SMILER

ART DIRECTORS/DESIGNERS | ELLEN SMILER,

CHERYL GILLIS

CLIENT | GILLIS & SMILER

PAPER/PRINTING | NEENAH CLASSIC

COLUMNS/THREE-COLOR OFFSET

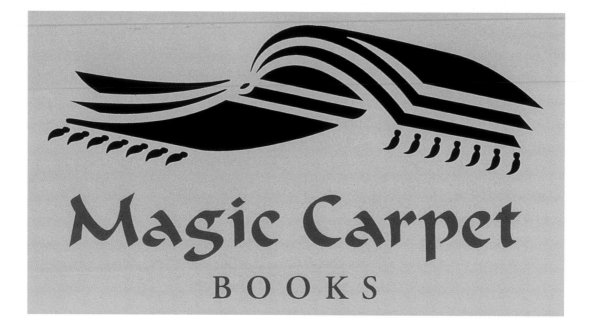

DESIGN FIRM | MIRES DESIGN
ART DIRECTOR | JOSÉ SERRANO
ILLUSTRATOR | TRACY SABIN
CLIENT | HARCOURT BRACE & COMPANY/MAGIC CARPET BOOKS
TOOLS | ADOBE ILLUSTRATOR

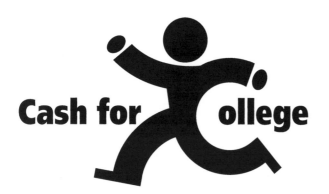

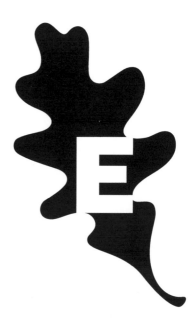

DESIGN FIRM | TIM NOONAN DESIGN
DESIGNER | TIM NOONAN
CLIENT | FIRSTAR BANK
TOOLS | ADOBE ILLUSTRATOR, QUARKXPRESS

DESIGN FIRM | MICHAEL STANARD DESIGN, INC.
ART DIRECTOR | MICHAEL STANARD
DESIGNERS | MICHAEL STANARD, KRISTY VANDEKERCKHOVE
ILLUSTRATOR | KRISTY VANDEKERCKHOVE
CLIENT | CITY OF EVANSTON
TOOLS | MACINTOSH, ADOBE ILLUSTRATOR

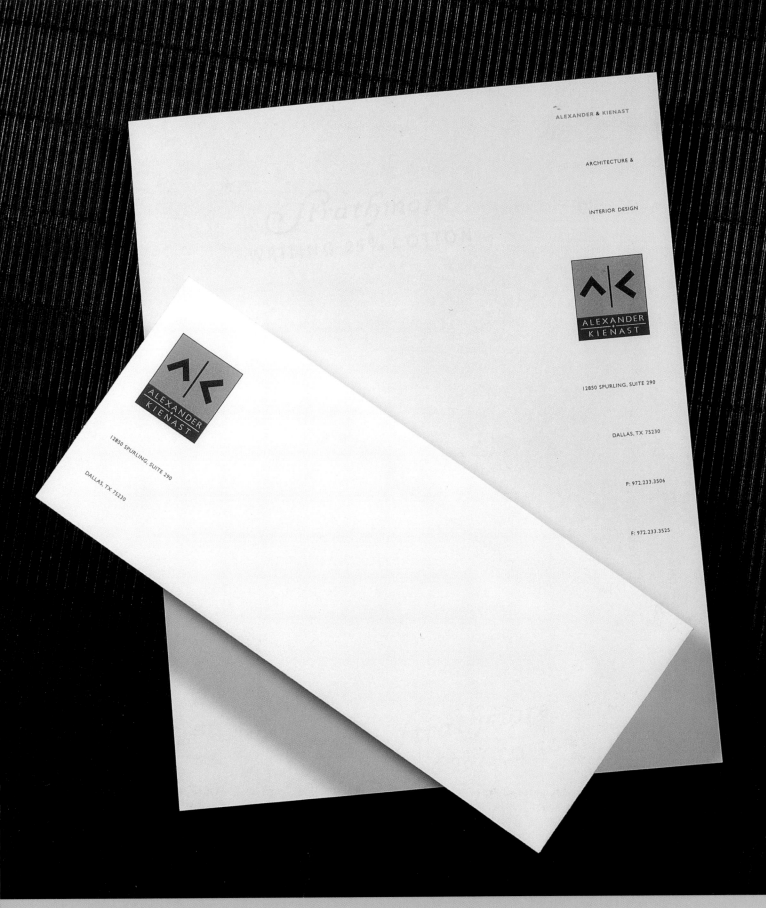

ALEXANDER & KIENAST

ARCHITECTURE &

INTERIOR DESIGN

12850 SPURLING, SUITE 290

DALLAS, TX 75230

P: 972.233.3506

F: 972.233.3525

ALEXANDER
KIENAST

12850 SPURLING, SUITE 290

DALLAS, TX 75230

DESIGN FIRM | SULLIVAN PERKINS
ART DIRECTOR/DESIGNER | MARCUS DICKERSON
CLIENT | ALEXANDER + KIENAST
TOOLS | MACINTOSH

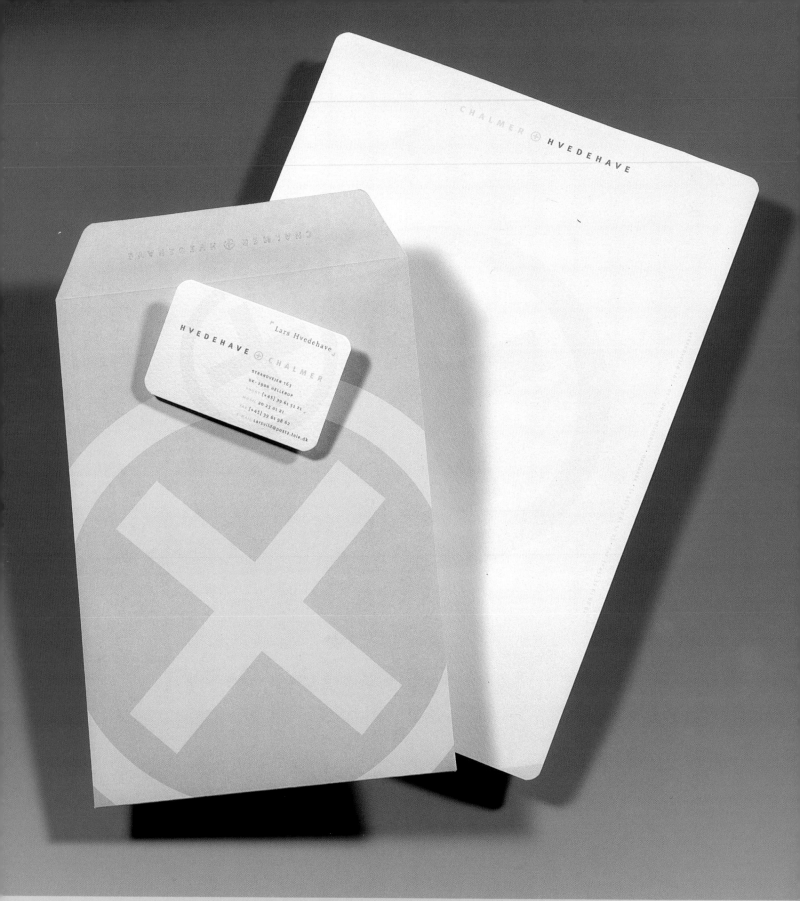

DESIGN FIRM | TRANSPARENT OFFICE

ART DIRECTOR/DESIGNER | VIBEKE NØDSKOV

CLIENT | CHALMER + HVEDEHAVE

TOOLS | QUARKXPRESS, ADOBE ILLUSTRATOR

PAPER/PRINTING | FAUNA RC 100G. IVORY/COLOR IT GREY

**GLOBALSERVE**

**GLOBALSERVE**

**The GlobalServe Corporation**
Park Plaza    1111 Chester Avenue    Suite 800
Cleveland Ohio  44114

**William Conrad**

**GLOBALSERVE**

**The GlobalServe Corporation**    Park Plaza
1111 Chester Avenue    Suite 800    Cleveland Ohio  44114
pager 216 890 3114    voice 216 579 1560
fax 216 579 0509
internet wconrad.globalserve@lnn.com

The GlobalServe Corporation    Park Plaza    1111 Chester Avenue    Suite 800    Cleveland   Ohio    44114   fax 216 579 0509    voice 216 579 1560

DESIGN FIRM | NESNADNY + SCHWARTZ

ALL DESIGN | GREGORY OZNOWICH

CLIENT | THE GLOBALSERVE CORPORATION

PAPER/PRINTING | MANADNOCK

STROLITE/HEXAGRAPHICS

DESIGN FIRM | VOSS DESIGN

ART DIRECTOR/DESIGNER | AXEL VOSS

CLIENT | CURT RICHTER FANIA, ARTIST-AGENCY

PAPER/PRINTING | GMUND SILENCIUM

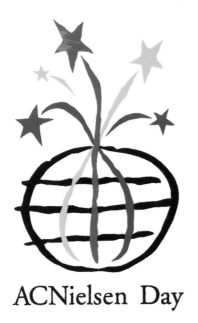

## ACNielsen Day

**DESIGN FIRM** | WEBSTER DESIGN ASSOCIATES
**ART DIRECTOR** | DAVE WEBSTER
**DESIGNER/ILLUSTRATOR** | ANDREY NAGORNEY
**CLIENT** | ACNIELSEN
**TOOLS** | ADOBE ILLUSTRATOR

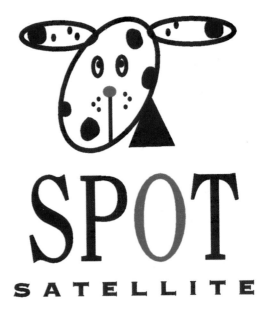

**DESIGN FIRM** | BARBARA BROWN MARKETING & DESIGN
**ART DIRECTOR/DESIGNER** | BARBARA BROWN
**CLIENT** | SPOT SATELLITE

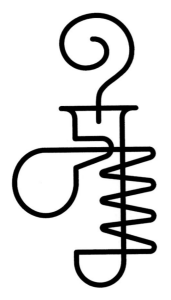

**DESIGN FIRM** | DESIGN CENTER
**ART DIRECTOR** | JOHN REGER
**DESIGNER** | SHERWIN SCHWARTZROCK
**CLIENT** | MCGINLEY ASSOCIATES
**TOOLS** | MACINTOSH

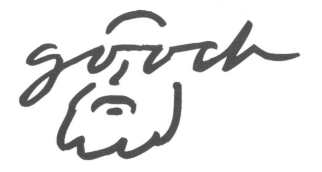

**DESIGN FIRM** | DOGSTAR
**DESIGNER/ILLUSTRATOR** | RODNEY DAVIDSON
**CLIENT** | MARK GOOCH PHOTOGRAPHY
**TOOLS** | ADOBE ILLUSTRATOR, STREAMLINE, MACROMEDIA FREEHAND

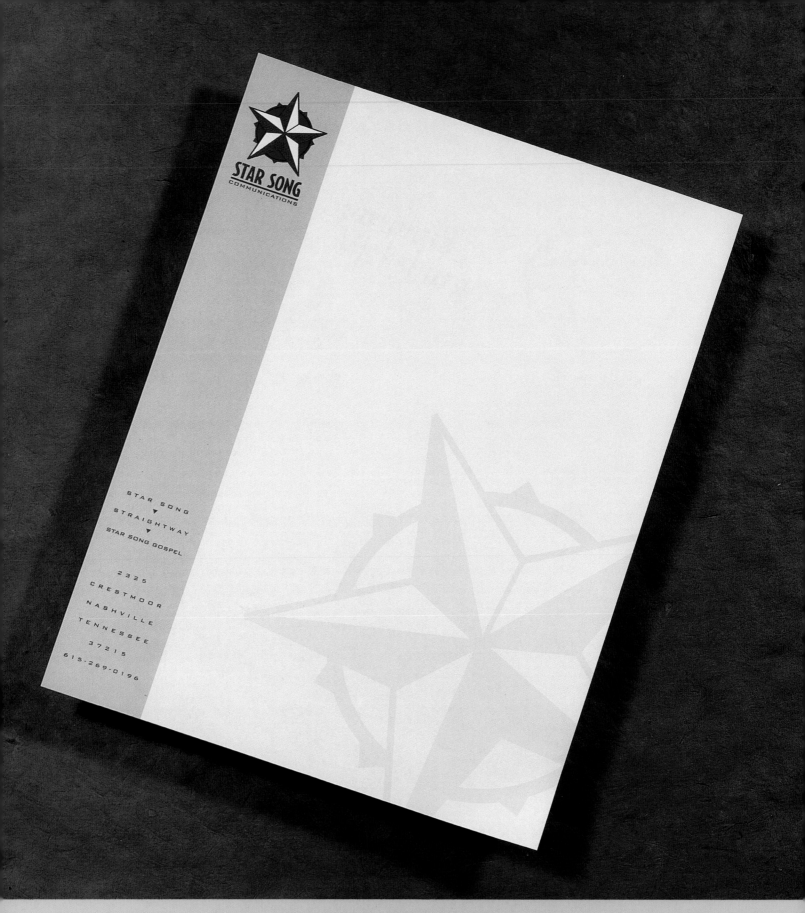

STAR SONG
▼
STRAIGHTWAY
▼
STAR SONG GOSPEL

2325
CRESTMOOR
NASHVILLE
TENNESSEE
37215
615-269-0196

STAR SONG
COMMUNICATIONS

DESIGN FIRM | AXIS DESIGN
ART DIRECTOR/DESIGNER | WILLIAM MILNAZIK
CLIENT | IMPACT TECHNOLOGY LTD.
PAPER/PRINTING | INKS: BLACK/PMS 123

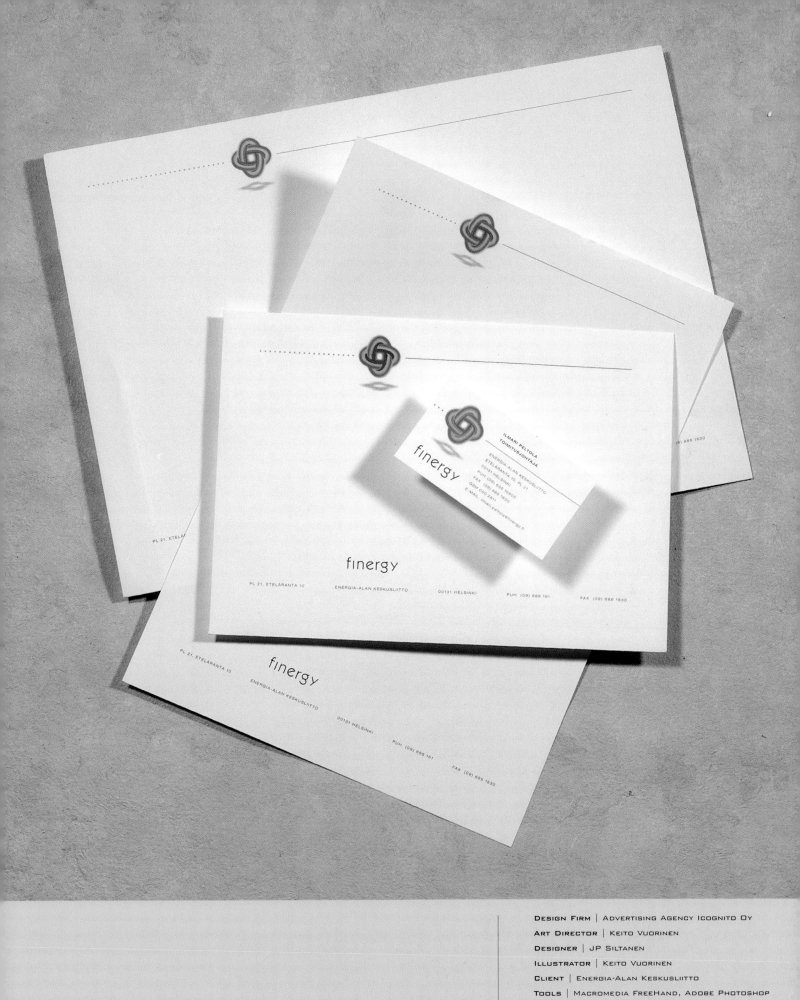

**Design Firm** | Advertising Agency Icognito Oy

**Art Director** | Keito Vuorinen

**Designer** | JP Siltanen

**Illustrator** | Keito Vuorinen

**Client** | Energia-Alan Keskusliitto

**Tools** | Macromedia FreeHand, Adobe Photoshop

**Paper/Printing** | F. G. Lönnberg

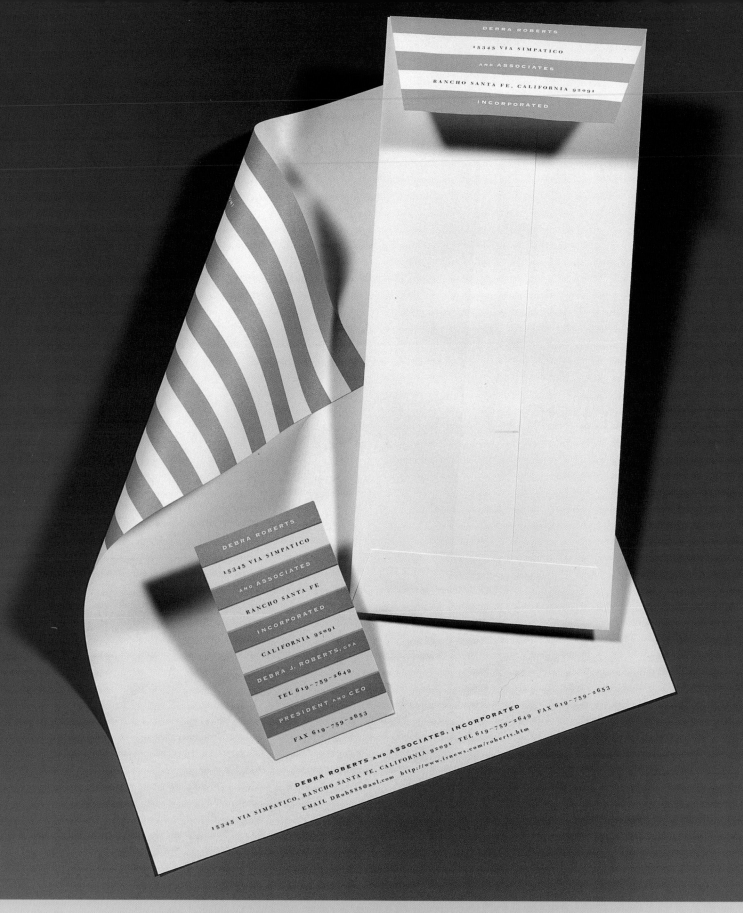

DEBRA ROBERTS
15345 VIA SIMPATICO
AND ASSOCIATES
RANCHO SANTA FE, CALIFORNIA 92091
INCORPORATED

DEBRA ROBERTS
15345 VIA SIMPATICO
AND ASSOCIATES
RANCHO SANTA FE
INCORPORATED
CALIFORNIA 92091
DEBRA J. ROBERTS, CFA
TEL 619-759-2649
PRESIDENT AND CEO
FAX 619-759-2653

DEBRA ROBERTS AND ASSOCIATES, INCORPORATED
15345 VIA SIMPATICO, RANCHO SANTA FE, CALIFORNIA 92091  TEL 619-759-2649  FAX 619-759-2653
EMAIL DRob888@aol.com  http://www.isnews.com/roberts.htm

DESIGN FIRM | MIRES DESIGN
ART DIRECTOR | SCOTT MIRES
DESIGNERS | DEBORAH HORN, SCOTT MIRES
CLIENT | DEBRA ROBERTS AND ASSOCIATES

DESIGN FIRM | MICHAEL STANARD DESIGN, INC.

ART DIRECTOR | MICHAEL STANARD

DESIGNER | KRISTY VANDEKERCKHOVE

CLIENT | JOHN MANCINI

TOOLS | MACINTOSH, ADOBE ILLUSTRATOR

PAPER/PRINTING | STRATHMORE WRITING

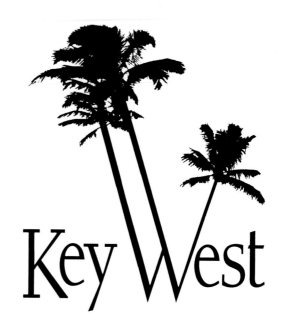

**DESIGN FIRM** | JEFF FISHER LOGOMOTIVES

**ALL DESIGN** | JEFF FISHER

**CLIENT** | JEFF MAUL, HAIR STYLIST

**TOOLS** | MACROMEDIA FREEHAND

**DESIGN FIRM** | MACVICAR DESIGN & COMMUNICATIONS

**ALL DESIGN** | WILLIAM A. GORDON

**CLIENT** | FEDERAL DATA CORPORATION

**TOOLS** | PEN, INK; ADOBE ILLUSTRATOR

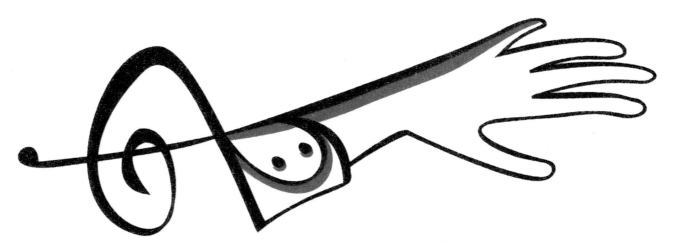

Vladimir Svoysky

**DESIGN FIRM** | CECILY ROBERTS DESIGN

**ALL DESIGN** | CECILY ROBERTS

**CLIENT** | VLADIMIR SVOYSKY

**TOOLS** | MACROMEDIA FREEHAND, QUARKXPRESS

**PAPER/PRINTING** | 80 LB. COVER ESSE, WHITE SMOOTH

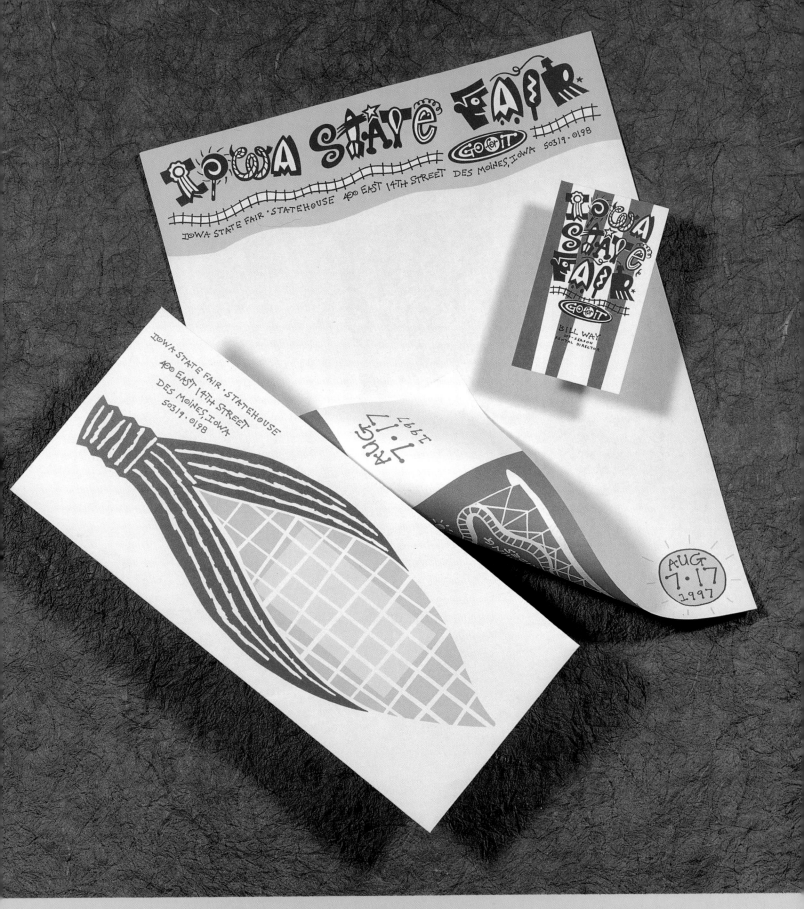

DESIGN FIRM | SAYLES GRAPHIC DESIGN
ART DIRECTOR/ILLUSTRATOR | JOHN SAYLES
DESIGNER | JOHN SAYLES, JENNIFER ELLIOTT
CLIENT | IOWA STATE FAIR

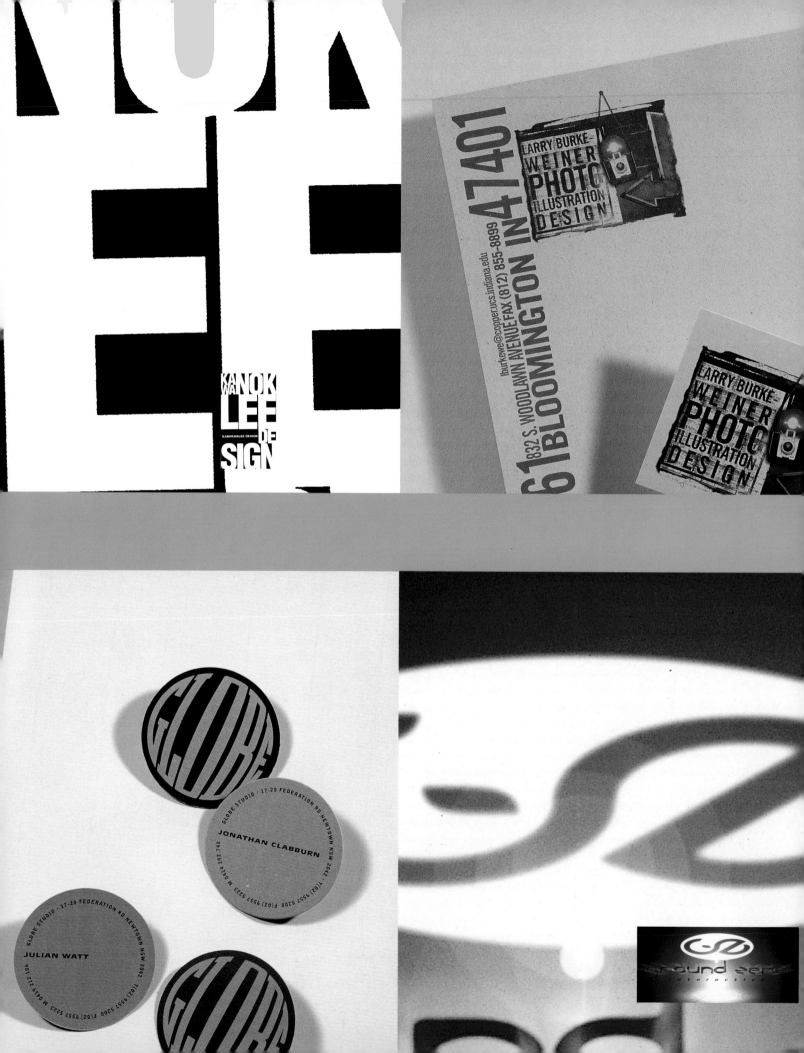

KANOKWAN
NOK
LEE
DE
SIGN

KANOKWALEE DESIGN

832 S. WOODLAWN AVENUE
lburkewe@copper.ucs.indiana.edu
FAX (812) 855-8899
BLOOMINGTON IN 47401
61

LARRY BURKE
WEINER
PHOTO
ILLUSTRATION
DESIGN

LARRY BURKE
WEINER
PHOTO
ILLUSTRATION
DESIGN

GLOBE

GLOBE STUDIO · 17-20 FEDERATION RD NEWTOWN NSW 2042
JONATHAN CLABBURN
T(02) 9557 5200  F(02) 9557 5223  M 0419 292 740

GLOBE STUDIO · 17-20 FEDERATION RD NEWTOWN NSW 2042
JULIAN WATT
T(02) 9557 5200  F(02) 9557 5223  M 0419 292 706

GLOBE

around zero
interactive

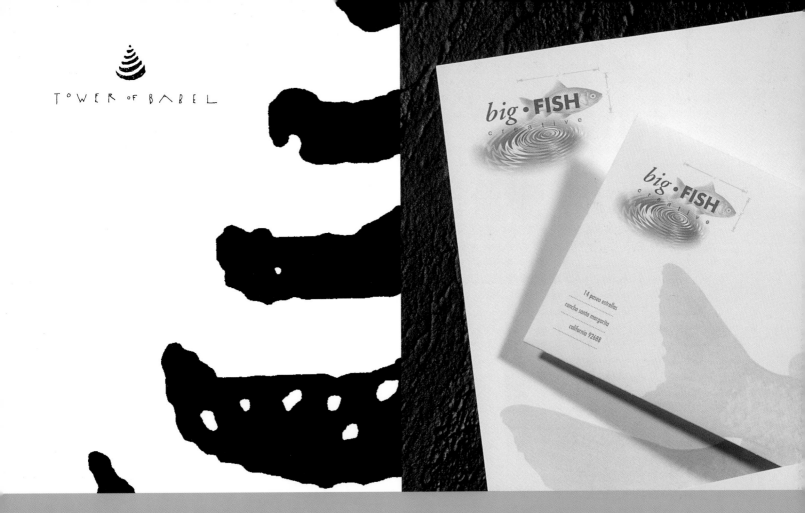

TOWER OF BABEL

big•FISH
creative

14 paseo estrellas

rancho santa margarita

california 92688

## CREATIVE SERVICES

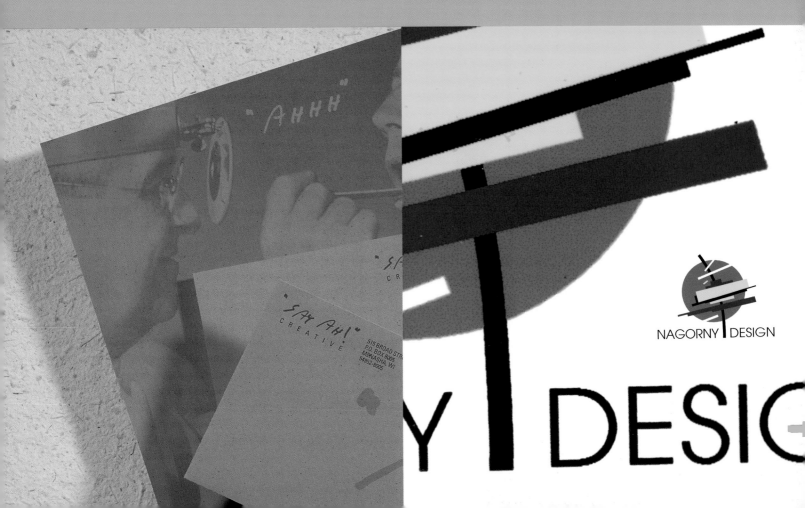

"AHHH"

SAY AH!
CREATIVE

SAY AH!
CREATIVE

515 BROAD STR
P.O. BOX 8005
MENASHA, WI
54952-8005

NAGORNY DESIGN

Y DESIG

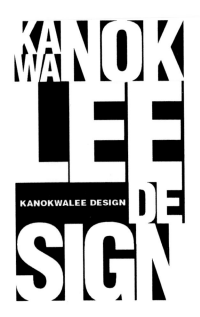

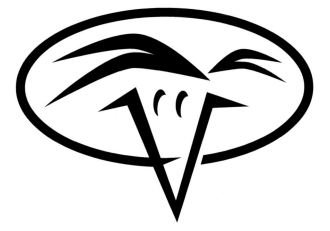

DESIGN FIRM | KANOKWALEE DESIGN

ART DIRECTOR/DESIGNER | KANOKWALEE LEE

CLIENT | KANOKWALEE DESIGN

TOOLS | ADOBE ILLUSTRATOR, QUARKXPRESS

DESIGN FIRM | GET SMART DESIGN COMPANY

DESIGNER/ILLUSTRATOR | TOM CULBERTSON

CLIENT | JODY VANDERAH/"V" MAN

TOOLS | MACROMEDIA FREEHAND

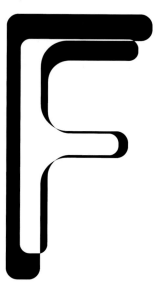

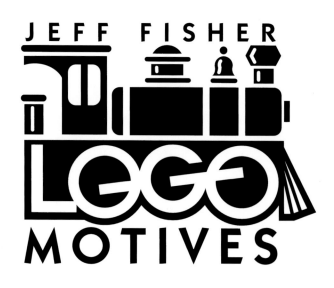

DESIGN FIRM | FORDESIGN

ALL DESIGN | FRANK FORD

CLIENT | FORDESIGN

TOOLS | ADOBE ILLUSTRATOR

DESIGN FIRM | JEFF FISHER LOGOMOTIVES

ALL DESIGN | JEFF FISHER

CLIENT | LOGOMOTIVES

TOOLS | MACROMEDIA FREEHAND

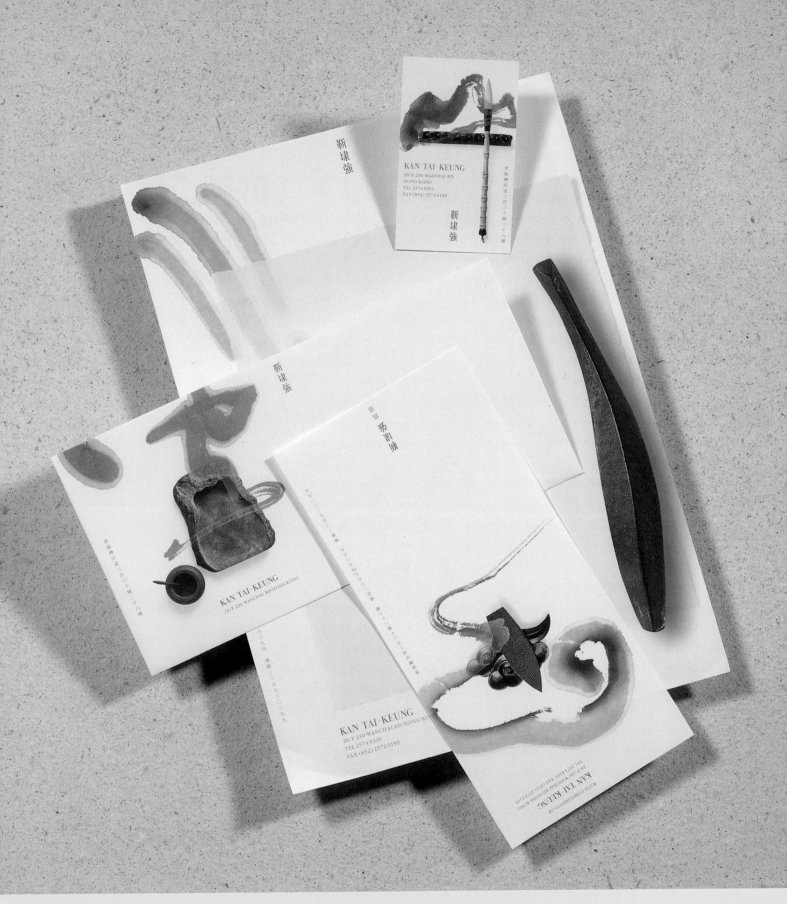

DESIGN FIRM | KAN & LAU DESIGN CONSULTANTS

ART DIRECTOR/DESIGNER | KAN TAI-KEUNG

CLIENT | KAN TAI-KEUNG

TOOLS | NAME CARD: CONQUEROR DIAMOND WHITE

CX22 250GSM; LETTERHEAD: CONQUEROR

DIAMOND WHITE CX22 100GSM; ENVELOPE:

CONQUEROR HIGHWHITE WOVE 100GSM/OFFSET

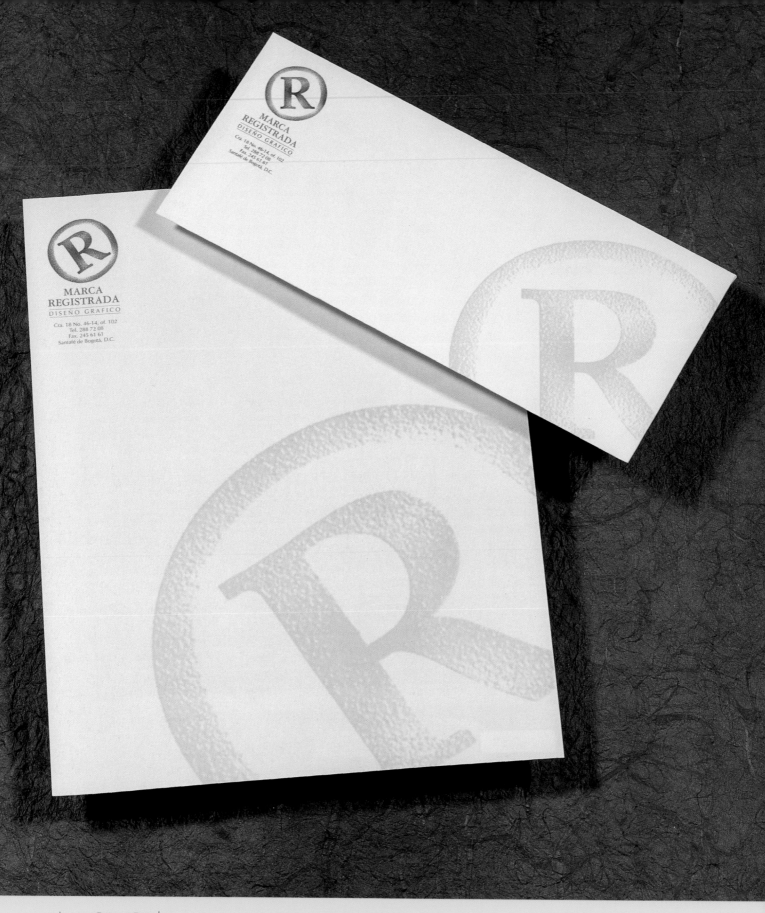

**DESIGN FIRM** | MARCA REGISTRADA DISEÑO GRAFICO

**ART DIRECTOR** | IVÁN CORREA

**DESIGNER** | MARTHA CADENA

**ILLUSTRATOR** | HENRY GONZÁLEZ

**CLIENT** | MARCA REGISTRADA DISEÑO GRAFICO

**TOOLS** | ADOBE PHOTOSHOP, MACINTOSH

**PAPER/PRINTING** | EDICIONES ANTROPOS (TORREÓN OFFSET)

GAF
ADVERTISING
DESIGN

GREGG A. FLOYD

7215
HOLLY HILL
SUITE 102
DALLAS, TEXAS 75231
TEL 214-360-9677
FAX 214-360-9678

**GAF ADVERTISING/DESIGN** 7215 HOLLY HILL, SUITE 102  DALLAS, TEXAS 75231

**GAF ADVERTISING/DESIGN**
7215 HOLLY HILL, SUITE 102 DALLAS, TEXAS 75231 TEL: 214-360-9677 FAX: 214-360-9678

DESIGN FIRM | GAF ADVERTISING DESIGN

ALL DESIGN | GREGG A. FLOYD

CLIENT | GAF ADVERTISING DESIGN

TOOLS | WOODCUT, QUARKXPRESS

PAPER/PRINTING | CONCRET/TWO COLOR SPOT LITHO

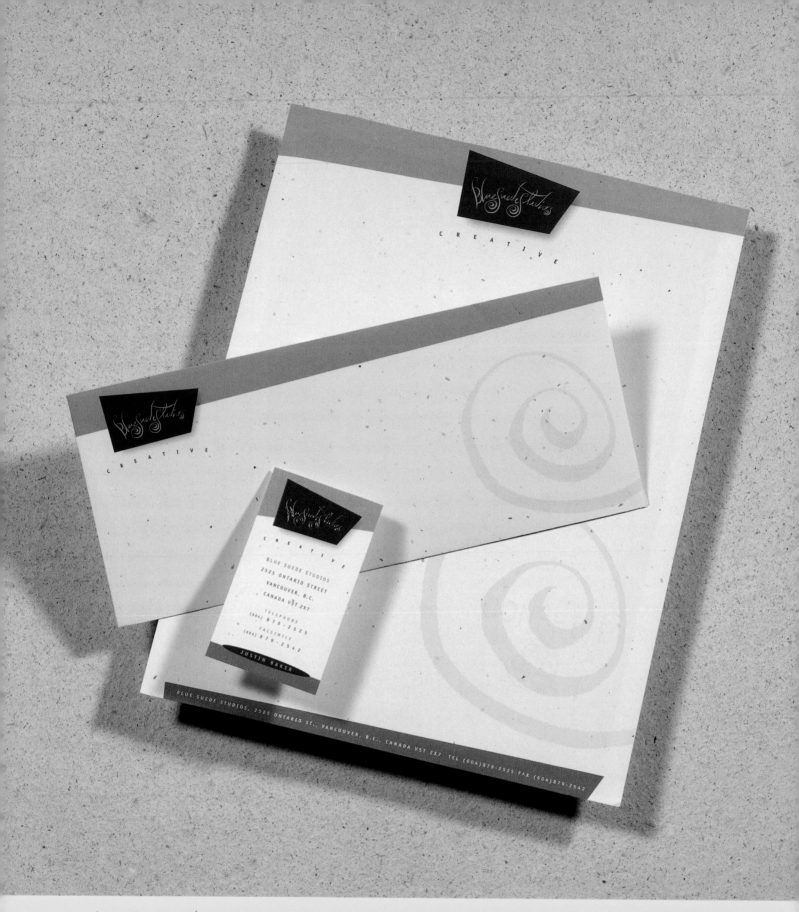

DESIGN FIRM | BLUE SUEDE STUDIOS
ART DIRECTOR | DAVE KENNEDY
DESIGNER/ILLUSTRATOR | JUSTIN BAKER
CLIENT | BLUE SUEDE STUDIOS
PAPER/PRINTING | CONFETTI/ULTRATECH PRINTERS

**DESIGN FIRM** | ABLE DESIGN, INC.

**ART DIRECTORS** | STUART HARVEY LEE, MARTHA DAVIS

**DESIGNER** | MARTIN PERRIN

**CLIENT** | ABLE DESIGN, INC.

**TOOLS** | POWER MACINTOSH, QUARKXPRESS

**PAPER/PRINTING** | BECKETT EXPRESSION, ICEBERG, 24 LB.

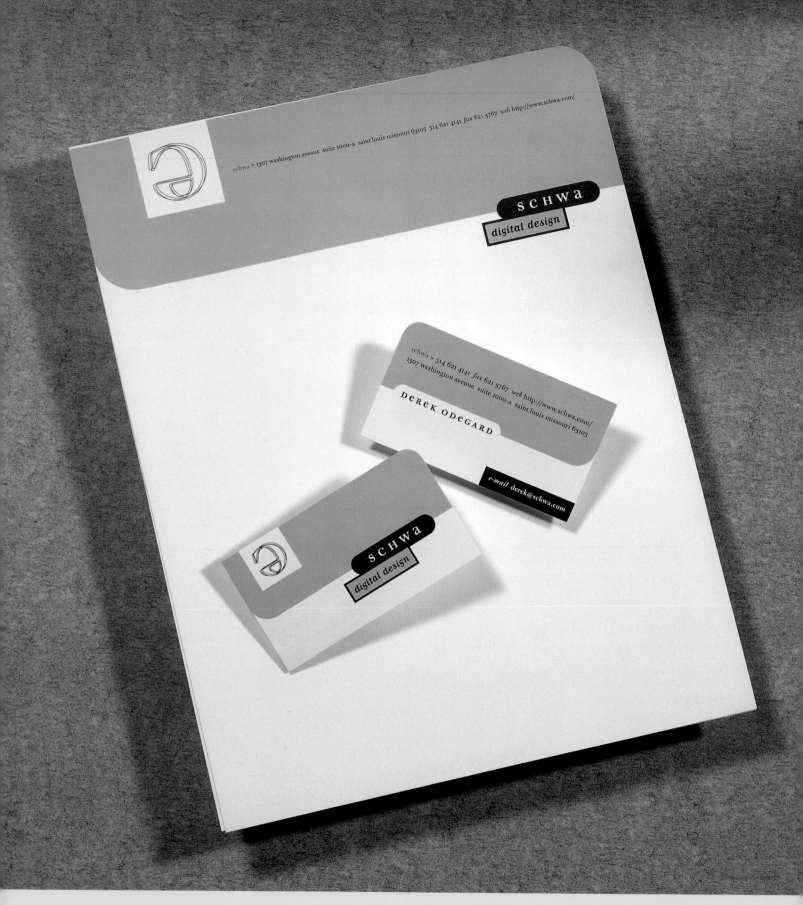

DESIGN FIRM | PHOENIX CREATIVE
ART DIRECTOR | ERIC THOELKE
DESIGNERS/ILLUSTRATORS | ERIC THOELKE, STEVE WIENKE
CLIENT | SCHWA DIGITAL DESIGN
TOOLS | ADOBE ILLUSTRATOR, QUARKXPRESS

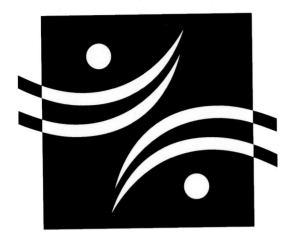

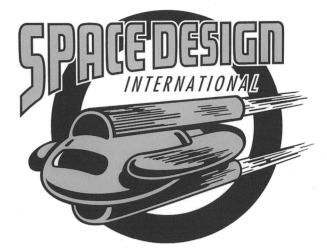

DESIGN FIRM | STEWART MONDERER DESIGN, INC.

ART DIRECTOR | STEWART MONDERER

DESIGNERS | AIME LECUSAY, STEWART MONDERER

ILLUSTRATOR | AIME LECUSAY

CLIENT | CORPORATE COMMUNICATIONS, INC.

TOOLS | ADOBE ILLUSTRATOR

DESIGN FIRM | SPACE DESIGN INTERNATIONAL

ALL DESIGN | TIM A. FRAME

CLIENT | SPACE DESIGN INTERNATIONAL

TOOLS | ADOBE ILLUSTRATOR

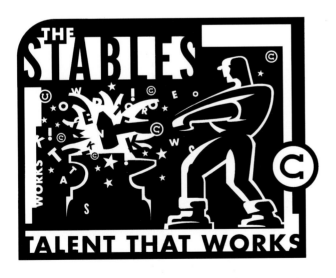

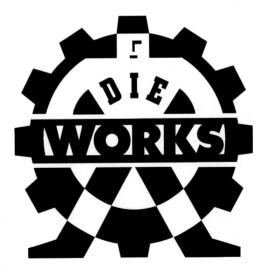

DESIGN FIRM | INSIGHT DESIGN COMMUNICATIONS

ALL DESIGN | SHERRIE HOLDEMAN, TRACY HOLDEMAN

CLIENT | THE STABLES

TOOLS | POWER MACINTOSH, MACROMEDIA FREEHAND

DESIGN FIRM | WEBSTER DESIGN ASSOCIATES

ART DIRECTOR | DAVE WEBSTER

DESIGNER/ILLUSTRATOR | ANDREY NAGORNY

CLIENT | DIE WORKS

TOOLS | MACROMEDIA FREEHAND

DESIGN FIRM | MULTIMEDIA ASIA, INC.

ART DIRECTOR | G. LEE

CLIENT | MULTIMEDIA ASIA, INC.

TOOLS | ADOBE PAGEMAKER

PAPER/PRINTING | 80 LB. MILKWEED GENESIS

DESIGN FIRM │ LARRY BURKE-WEINER DESIGN

ALL DESIGN │ LARRY BURKE-WEINER

CLIENT │ LARRY BURKE-WEINER

TOOLS │ ADOBE PHOTOSHOP, PAINTER,

ADOBE ILLUSTRATOR, QUARKXPRESS

DESIGN FIRM | BIG FISH CREATIVE

ALL DESIGN | THOMAS HAWTHORNE

CLIENT | BIG FISH CREATIVE

TOOLS | QUARKXPRESS, ADOBE PHOTOSHOP, MACINTOSH

PAPER/PRINTING | STRATHMORE ELEMENTS

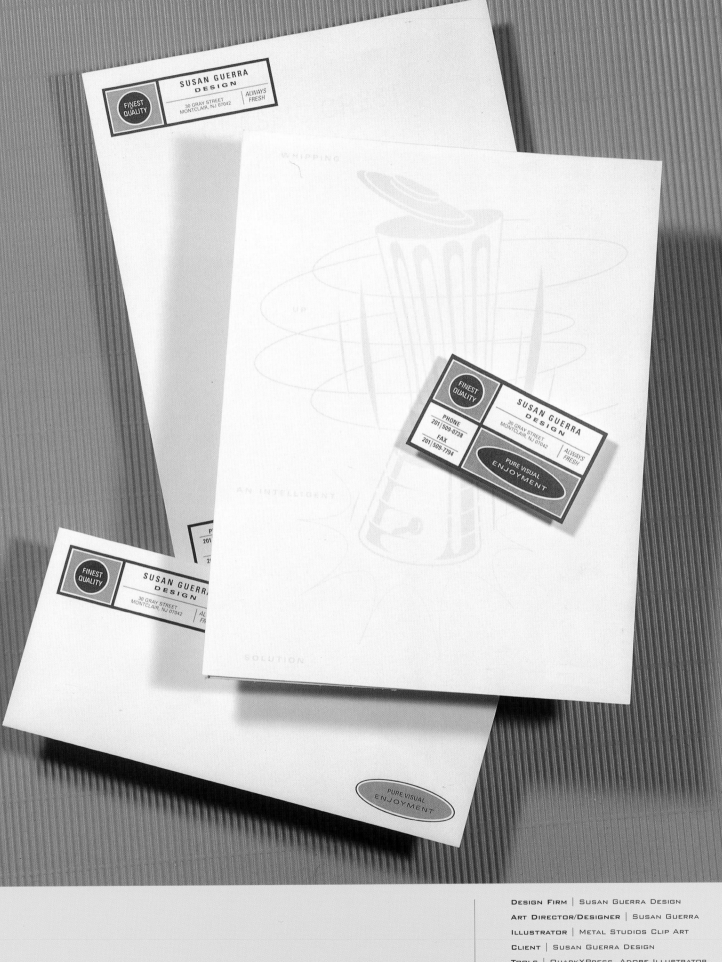

DESIGN FIRM | SUSAN GUERRA DESIGN

ART DIRECTOR/DESIGNER | SUSAN GUERRA

ILLUSTRATOR | METAL STUDIOS CLIP ART

CLIENT | SUSAN GUERRA DESIGN

TOOLS | QUARKXPRESS, ADOBE ILLUSTRATOR

PAPER/PRINTING | CLASSIC CREST/TWO COLOR

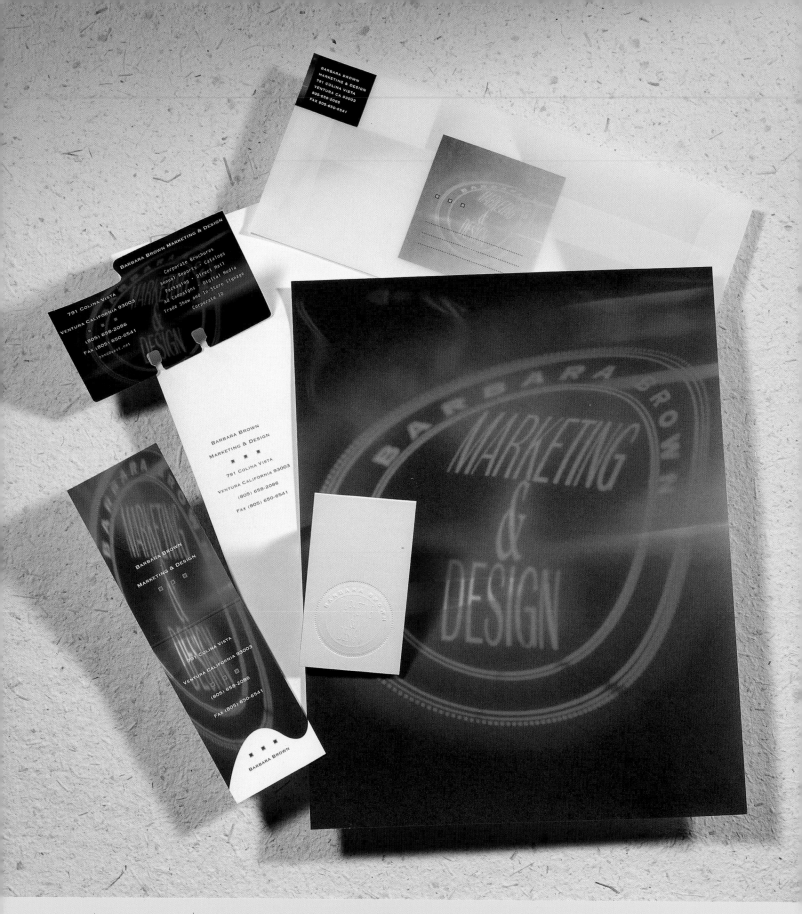

DESIGN FIRM | BARBARA BROWN MARKETING & DESIGN

ART DIRECTOR | BARBARA BROWN

DESIGNER | LANA CURTIN, PRODUCTION ARTIST

PHOTOGRAPHER | SCHAF PHOTO

CLIENT | BARBARA BROWN MARKETING & DESIGN

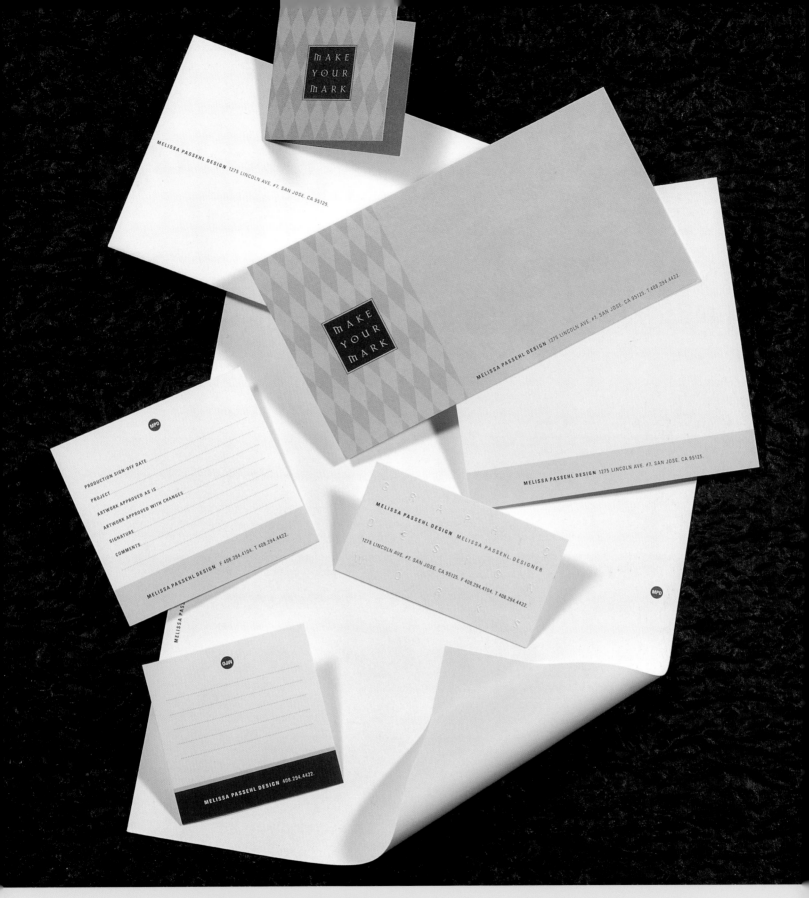

DESIGN FIRM | MELISSA PASSEHL DESIGN
ART DIRECTOR | MELISSA PASSEHL
DESIGNERS | MELISSA PASSEHL, CHARLOTTE LAMBRECHTS
CLIENT | MELISSA PASSEHL DESIGN

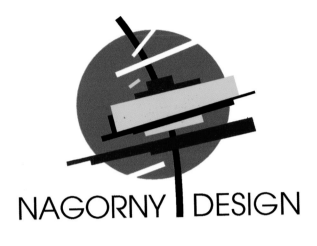

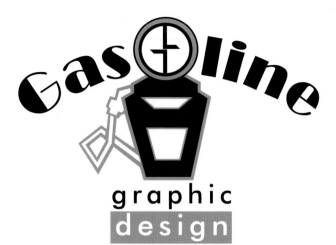

DESIGN FIRM | NAGORNY DESIGN
ALL DESIGN | ANDREY NAGORNY
CLIENT | NAGORNY DESIGN
TOOLS | MACROMEDIA FREEHAND

DESIGN FIRM | GASOLINE GRAPHIC DESIGN
ART DIRECTORS | ANGELINE BECKLEY, ZANE VREDENBURG
DESIGNERS | ZANE VREDENBURG, ANGELINE BECKLEY
CLIENT | GASOLINE GRAPHIC DESIGN
TOOLS | ADOBE ILLUSTRATOR

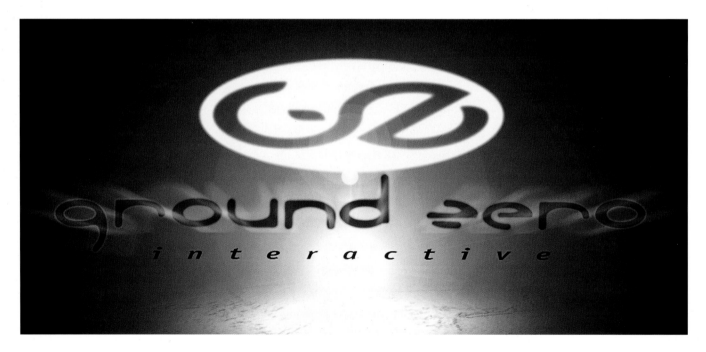

DESIGN FIRM | M8BIUS
ALL DESIGN | CHIP TAYLOR
CLIENT | GROUND ZERO INTERACTIVE
TOOLS | MACINTOSH, ADOBE PHOTOSHOP, ADOBE ILLUSTRATOR

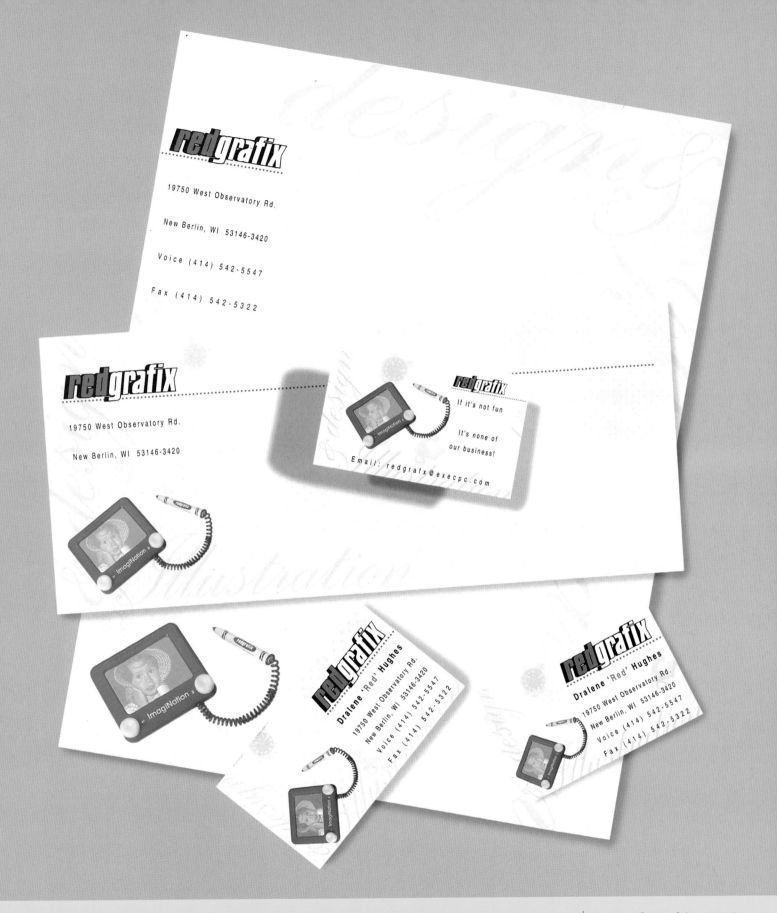

DESIGN FIRM | REDGRAFIX DESIGN & ILLUSTRATION

ALL DESIGN | DRALENE "RED" HUGHES

CLIENT | REDGRAFIX DESIGN & ILLUSTRATION

TOOLS | ADOBE PHOTOSHOP, ADOBE ILLUSTRATOR,
QUARKXPRESS

PAPER/PRINTING | STRATHMORE ELEMENTS
WHITE/FOUR COLOR, TI PRINTING

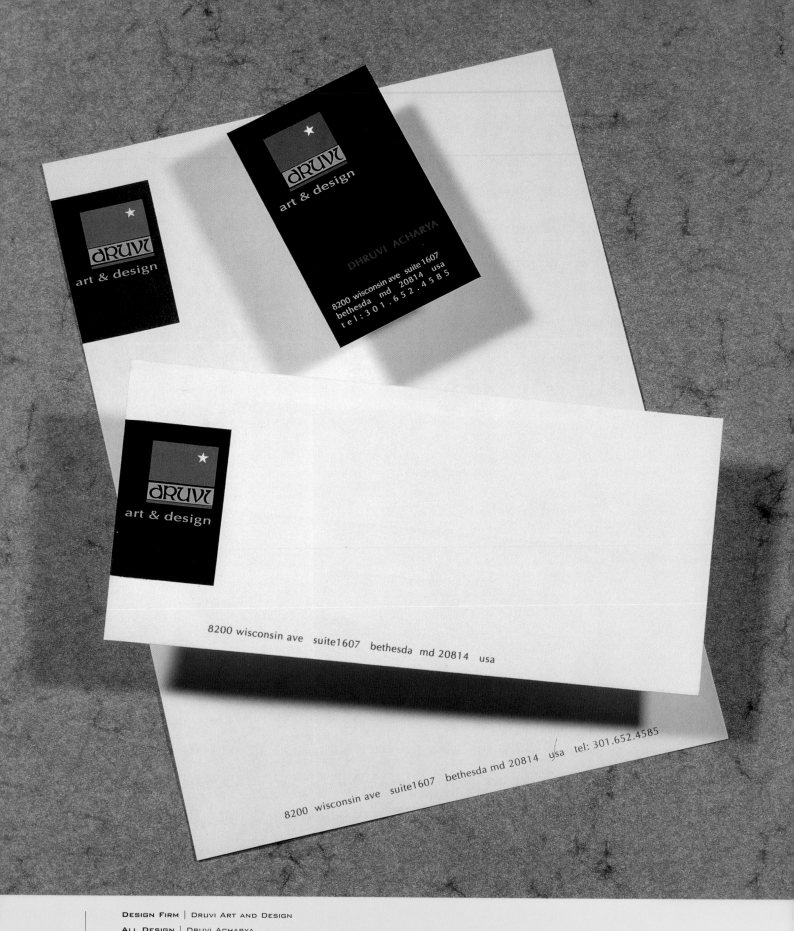

DESIGN FIRM | DRUVI ART AND DESIGN

ALL DESIGN | DRUVI ACHARYA

CLIENT | DRUVI ART AND DESIGN

PAPER/PRINTING | 80/100 LBS. CARD STOCK,
    BOND PAPER/SCREENPRINTING

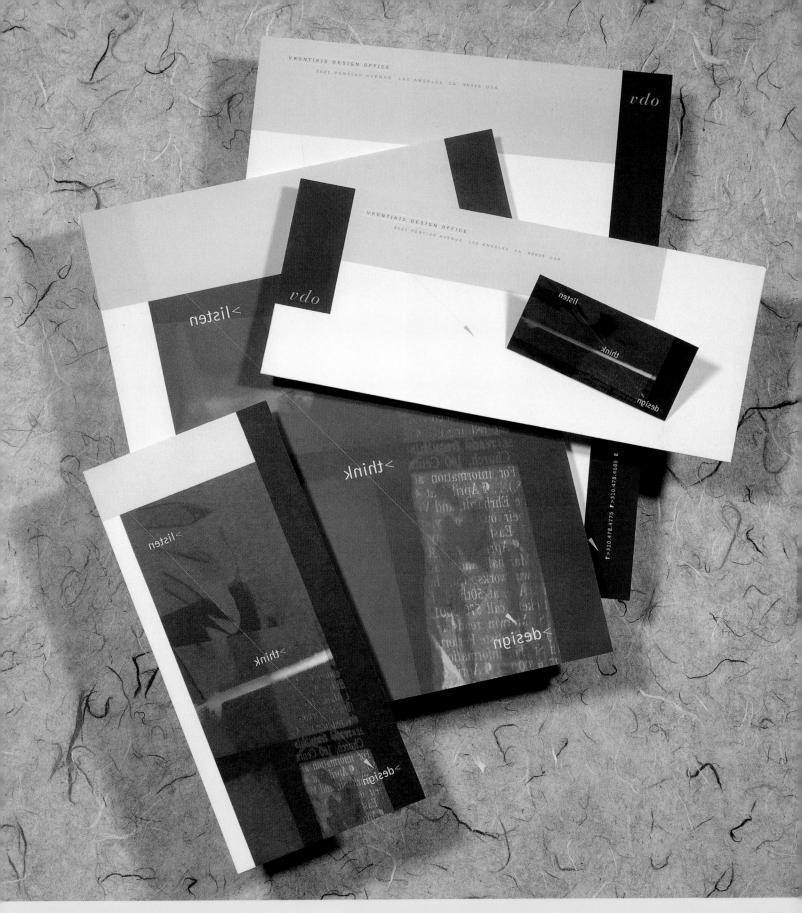

VRONTIKIS DESIGN OFFICE
2021 PONTIUS AVENUE LOS ANGELES CA 90025 USA

DESIGN FIRM | VRONTIKIS DESIGN OFFICE
ART DIRECTOR/DESIGNER | PETRULA VRONTIKIS
CLIENT | VRONTIKIS DESIGN OFFICE
TOOLS | QUARKXPRESS, ADOBE PHOTOSHOP
PAPER/PRINTING | NEENAH CLASSIC CREST/LOGIN PRINTING

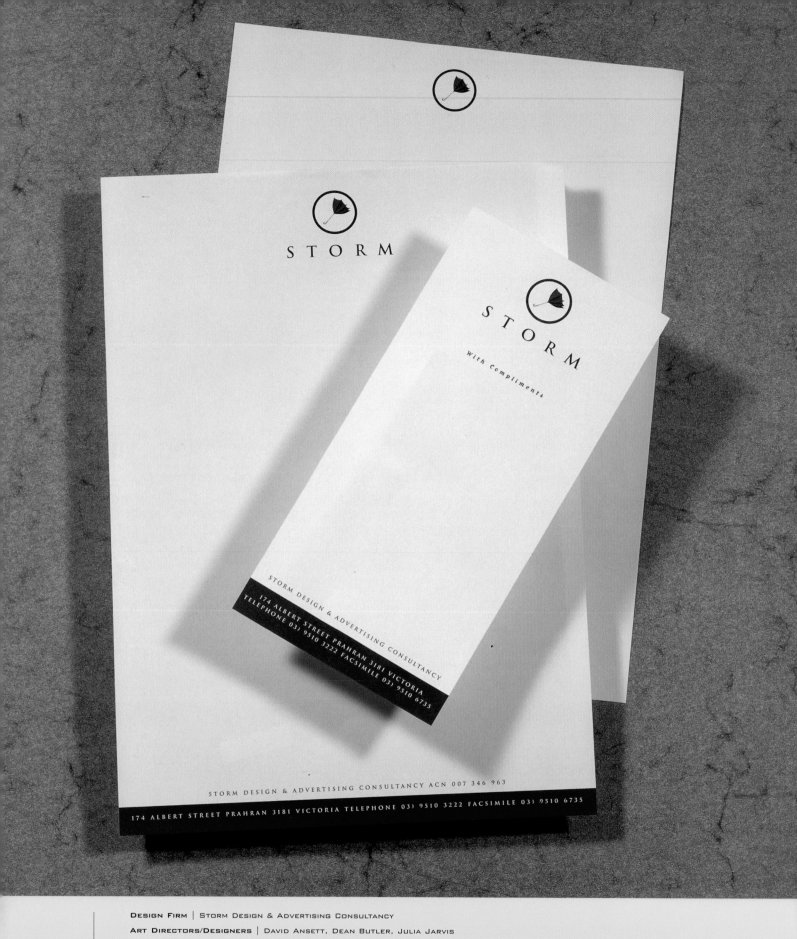

DESIGN FIRM | STORM DESIGN & ADVERTISING CONSULTANCY

ART DIRECTORS/DESIGNERS | DAVID ANSETT, DEAN BUTLER, JULIA JARVIS

PHOTOGRAPHER | MARCUS STRUZINA

CLIENT | STORM DESIGN & ADVERTISING CONSULTANCY

TOOLS | ADOBE PHOTOSHOP

PAPER/PRINTING | SAXTON SMOOTHE/FOUR COLOR PROCESS PLUS ONE

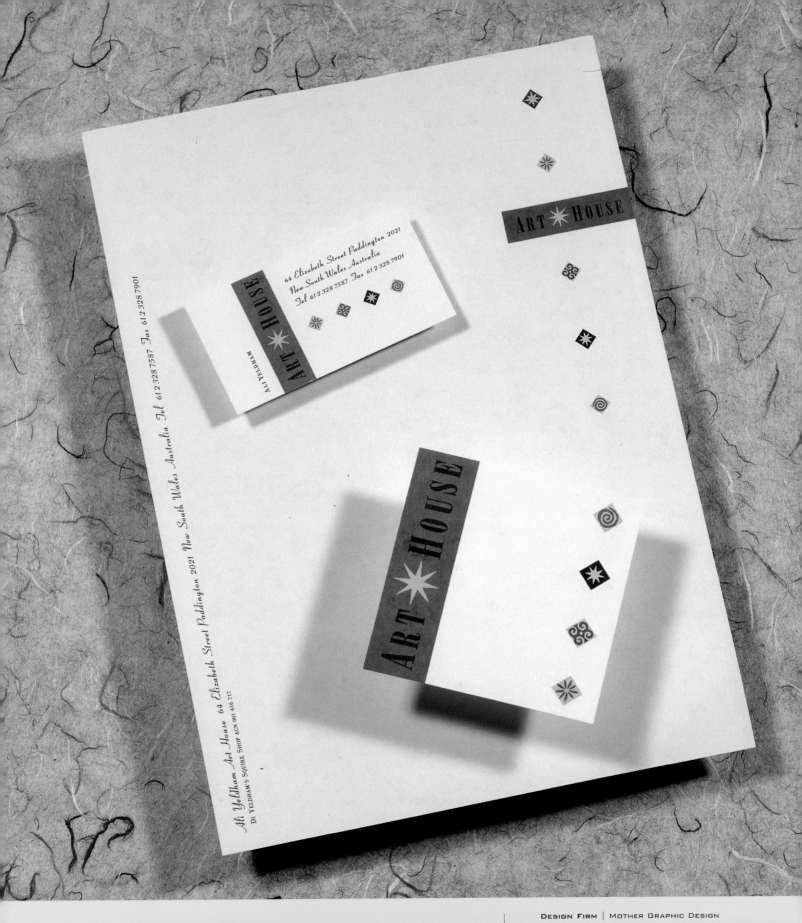

DESIGN FIRM | MOTHER GRAPHIC DESIGN

ALL DESIGN | KRISTIN THIEME

CLIENT | ART HOUSE

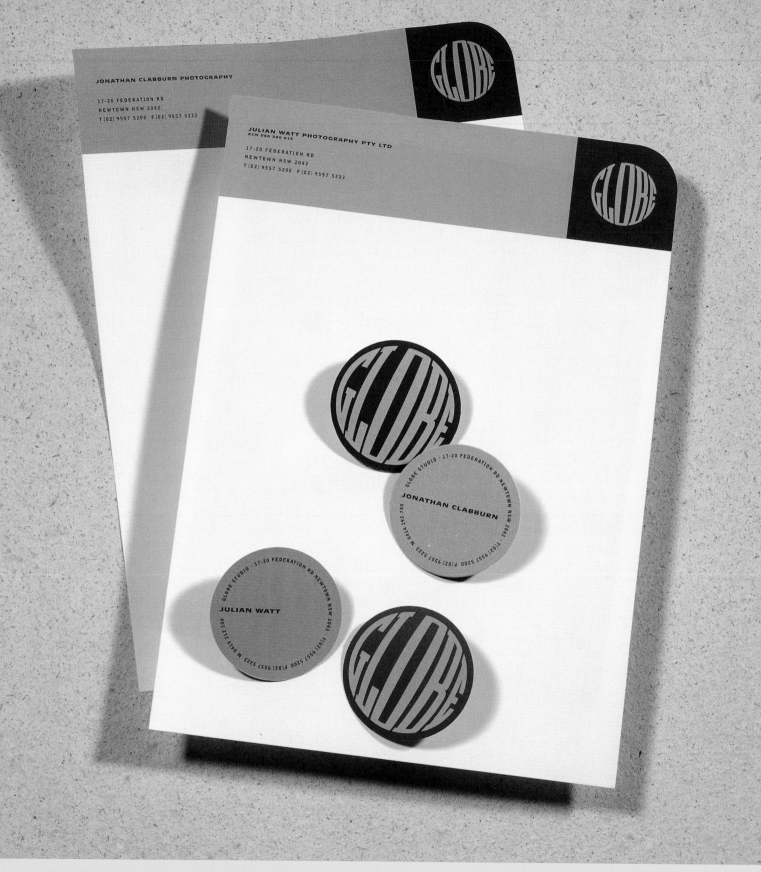

JONATHAN CLABBURN PHOTOGRAPHY

17-20 FEDERATION RD
NEWTOWN NSW 2042
T (02) 9557 5200  F (02) 9557 5223

JULIAN WATT PHOTOGRAPHY PTY LTD
ACN 056 590 813

17-20 FEDERATION RD
NEWTOWN NSW 2042
T (02) 9557 5200  F (02) 9557 5223

GLOBE STUDIO · 17-20 FEDERATION RD NEWTOWN NSW 2042
JONATHAN CLABBURN
T (02) 9557 5200  F (02) 9557 5223  M 0414 292 740

GLOBE STUDIO · 17-20 FEDERATION RD NEWTOWN NSW 2042
JULIAN WATT
T (02) 9557 5200  F (02) 9557 5223  M 0419 212 106

DESIGN FIRM | MOTHER GRAPHIC DESIGN
ART DIRECTOR/DESIGNER | KRISTIN THIEME
CLIENT | GLOBE STUDIO

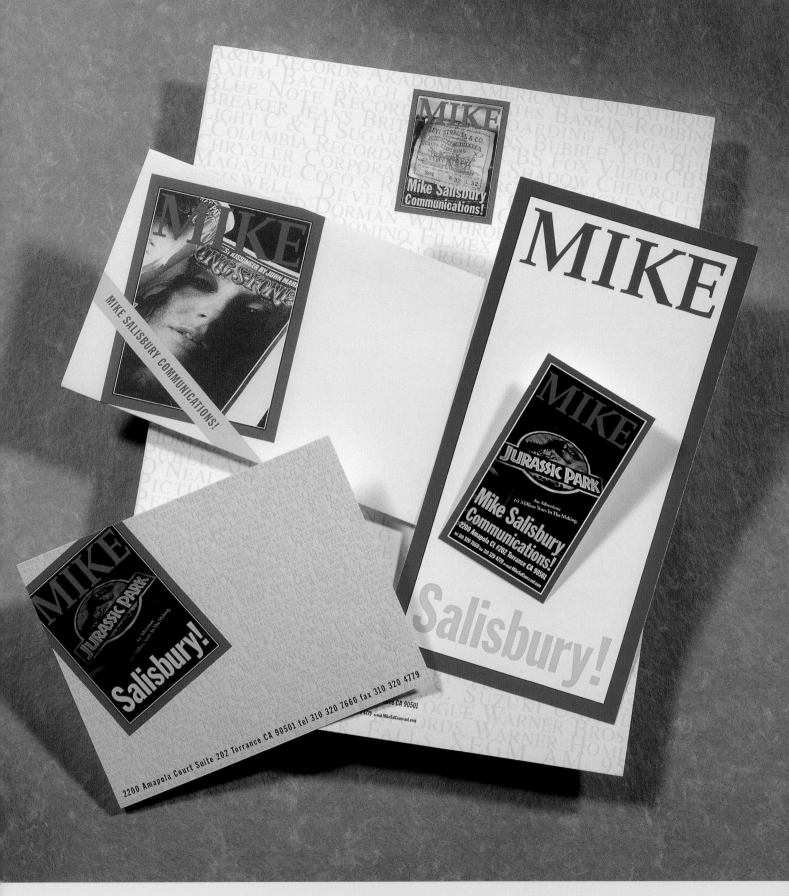

DESIGN FIRM | MIKE SALISBURY COMMUNICATIONS, INC.

ART DIRECTOR | MIKE SALISBURY

DESIGNER | MARY EVELYN MCGOUGH

CLIENT | MIKE SALISBURY COMMUNICATIONS

PLATINUM DESIGN, INC.
14 West 23rd St., New York, NY 10010
tel: 212-366-4000 fax: 212-366-4046

PLATINUM

PLATINUM DESIGN, INC.
14 West 23rd St., New York, NY 10010

PLATINUM

DESIGN FIRM | PLATINUM DESIGN, INC.

ART DIRECTOR/DESIGNER | VICTORIA STAMM

CLIENT | PLATINUM DESIGN, INC.

TOOLS | POWER MACINTOSH 8100

PAPER/PRINTING | CLR/STARWHITE VICKSBURG

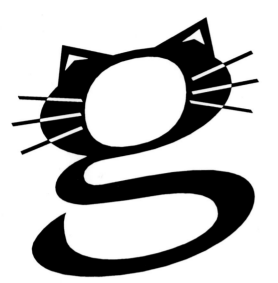

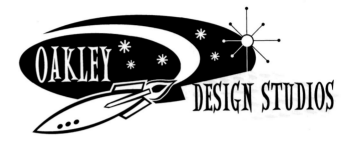

DESIGN FIRM | GRAY CAT DESIGN
DESIGNER | LISA SCALISE
CLIENT | GRAY CAT DESIGN
PAPER/PRINTING | MOHAWK SUPERFINE/LAKE PRINTERS

DESIGN FIRM | OAKLEY DESIGN STUDIOS
ALL DESIGN | TIM OAKLEY
CLIENT | OAKLEY DESIGN STUDIOS
TOOLS | ADOBE ILLUSTRATOR

# JUICE

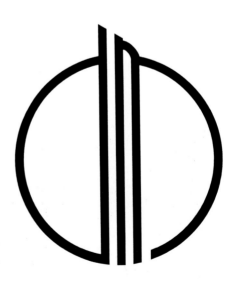

DESIGN FIRM | JUICE DESIGN
ART DIRECTOR | BRETT M. CRITCHLOW
DESIGNERS | BRETT M. CRITCHLOW, MATT SMIALEK, MIMI PAJO
CLIENT | JUICE DESIGN

DESIGN FIRM | MALIK DESIGN
ALL DESIGN | DONNA MALIK
CLIENT | MALIK DESIGN
TOOLS | MACROMEDIA FREEHAND
PAPER/PRINTING | STRATHMORE RENEWAL

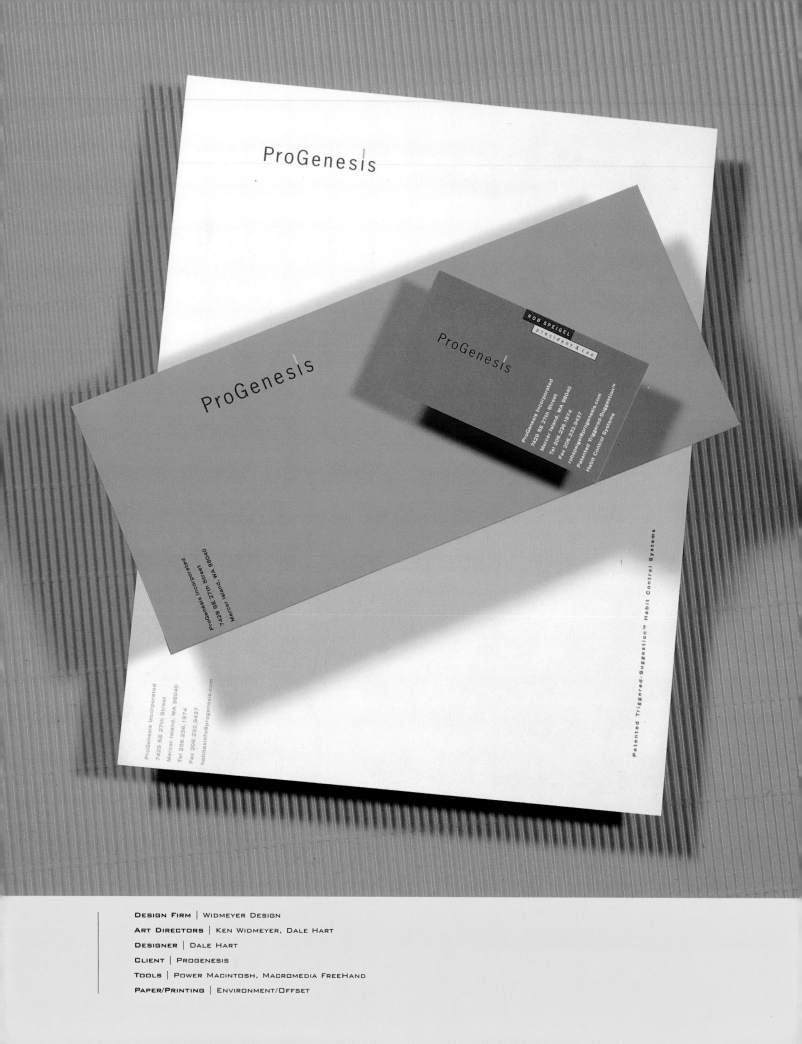

DESIGN FIRM | WIDMEYER DESIGN

ART DIRECTORS | KEN WIDMEYER, DALE HART

DESIGNER | DALE HART

CLIENT | PROGENESIS

TOOLS | POWER MACINTOSH, MACROMEDIA FREEHAND

PAPER/PRINTING | ENVIRONMENT/OFFSET

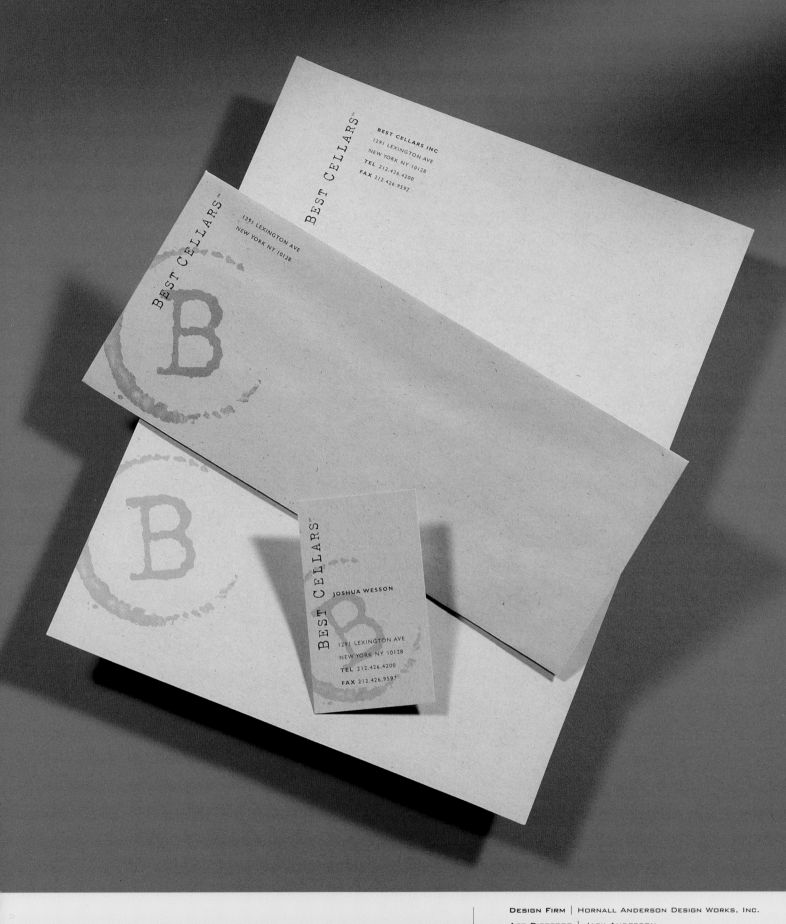

DESIGN FIRM | HORNALL ANDERSON DESIGN WORKS, INC.

ART DIRECTOR | JACK ANDERSON

DESIGNERS | JACK ANDERSON, LISA CERVENY,

JANA WILSON, DAVID BATES

CLIENT | BEST CELLARS

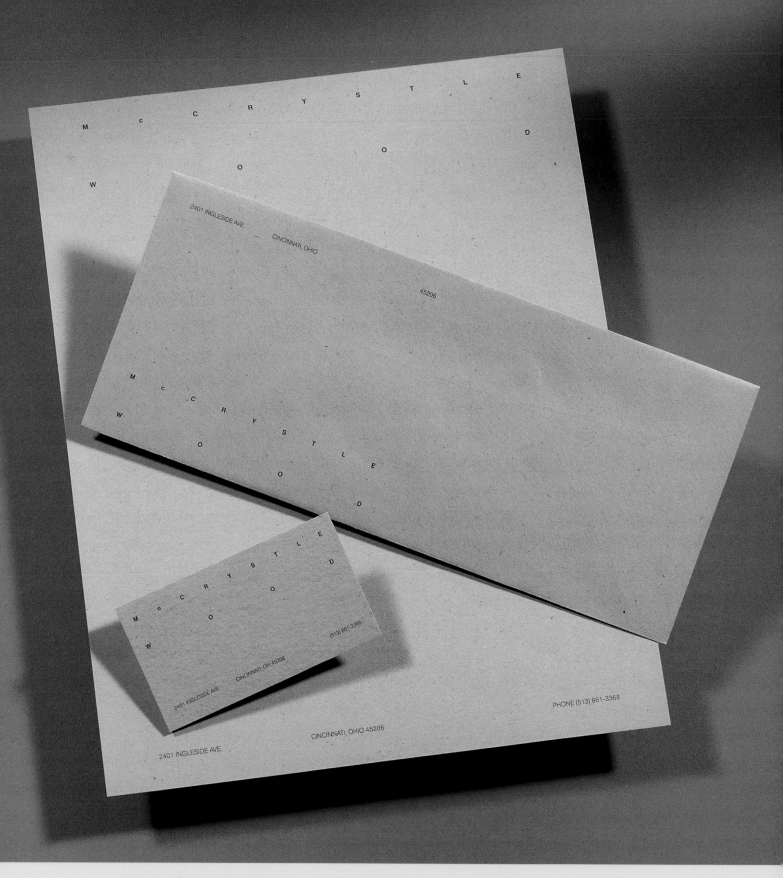

DESIGN FIRM | WOOD/BROD DESIGN

ART DIRECTOR/DESIGNER | STAN BROD

CLIENT | STAN BROD, McCRYSTLE WOOD

TOOLS | ADOBE ILLUSTRATOR

PAPER/PRINTING | SPECKLETONE/BERMAN PRINTING COMPANY

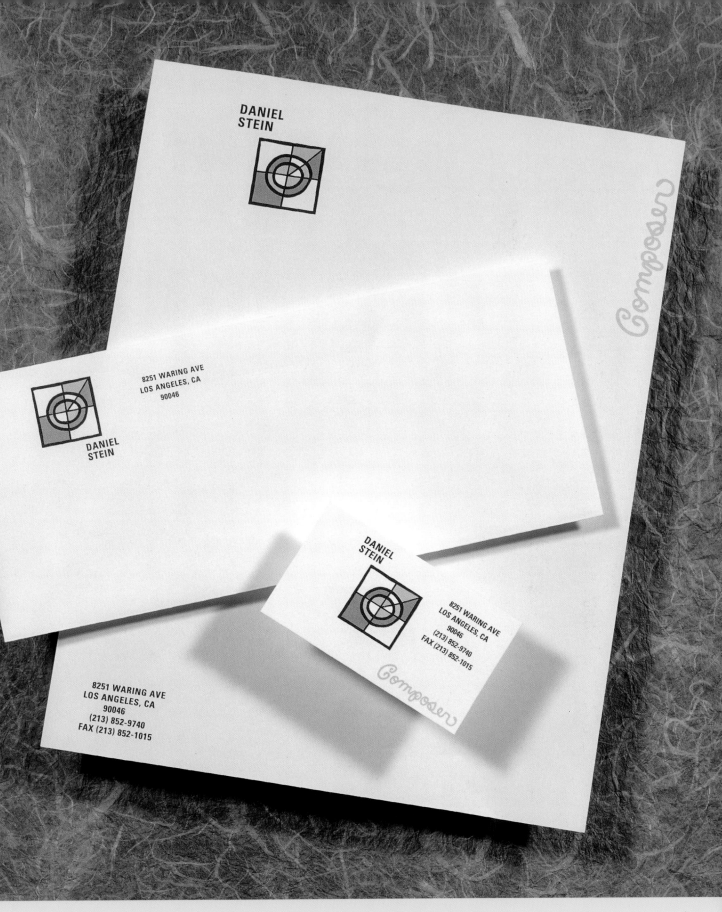

DESIGN FIRM | SUSAN GUERRA DESIGN

ALL DESIGN | SUSAN GUERRA DESIGN

CLIENT | DANIEL STEIN

TOOLS | ADOBE ILLUSTRATOR

PAPER/PRINTING | CLASSIC CREST/TWO COLOR

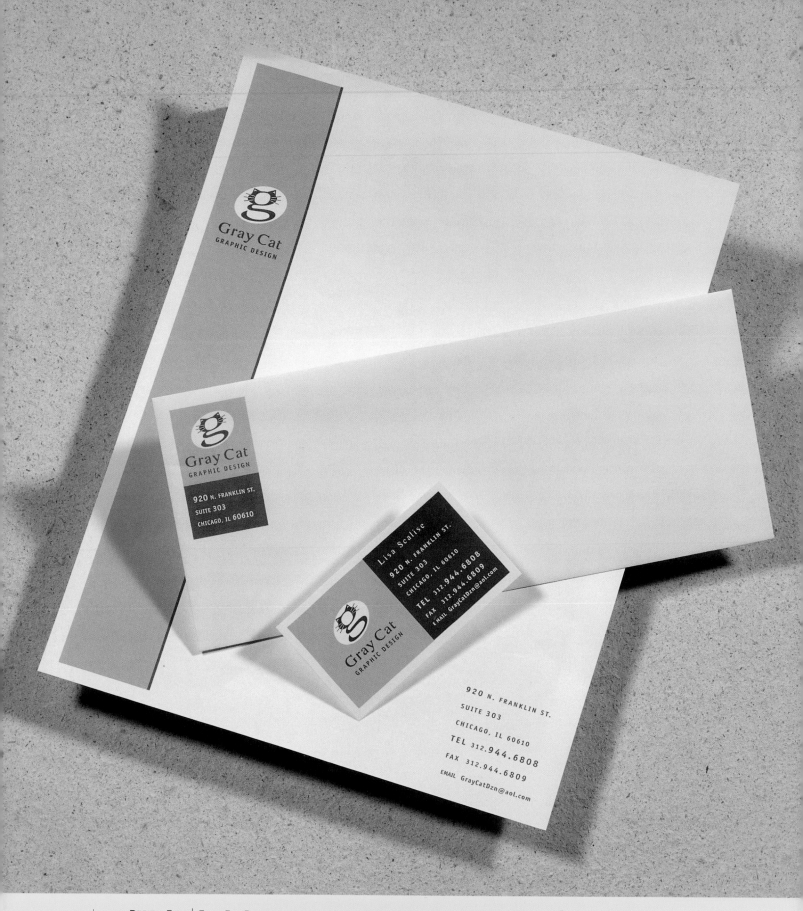

DESIGN FIRM | GRAY CAT DESIGN

DESIGNER | LISA SCALISE

CLIENT | GRAY CAT DESIGN

PAPER/PRINTING | MOHAWK SUPERFINE/LAKE PRINTERS

DESIGN FIRM | "SAY AH!" CREATIVE

ART DIRECTOR/DESIGNER | KELLY D. LAWRENCE

PHOTOGRAPHY | SUPERSTOCK

PRODUCTION | JON EMPEY, VICKIE MARTIN

CLIENT | "SAY AH!" CREATIVE

TOOLS | QUARKXPRESS, ADOBE PHOTOSHOP,
ADOBE ILLUSTRATOR

PAPER/PRINTING | SIMPSON QUEST-BRONZE/OFFSET

KANOK
WA
LEE
DE
SIGN

10402 YUCCA DRIVE · AUSTIN, TEXAS 78759

VOICE: 512-257-1566 FAX: 512-257-1496

**DESIGN FIRM** | KANOKWALEE DESIGN

**ART DIRECTOR/DESIGNER** | KANOKWALEE LEE

**CLIENT** | KANOKWALEE DESIGN

**TOOLS** | ADOBE ILLUSTRATOR, QUARKXPRESS

**PAPER/PRINTING** | STRATHMORE KRAFT/OFFSET

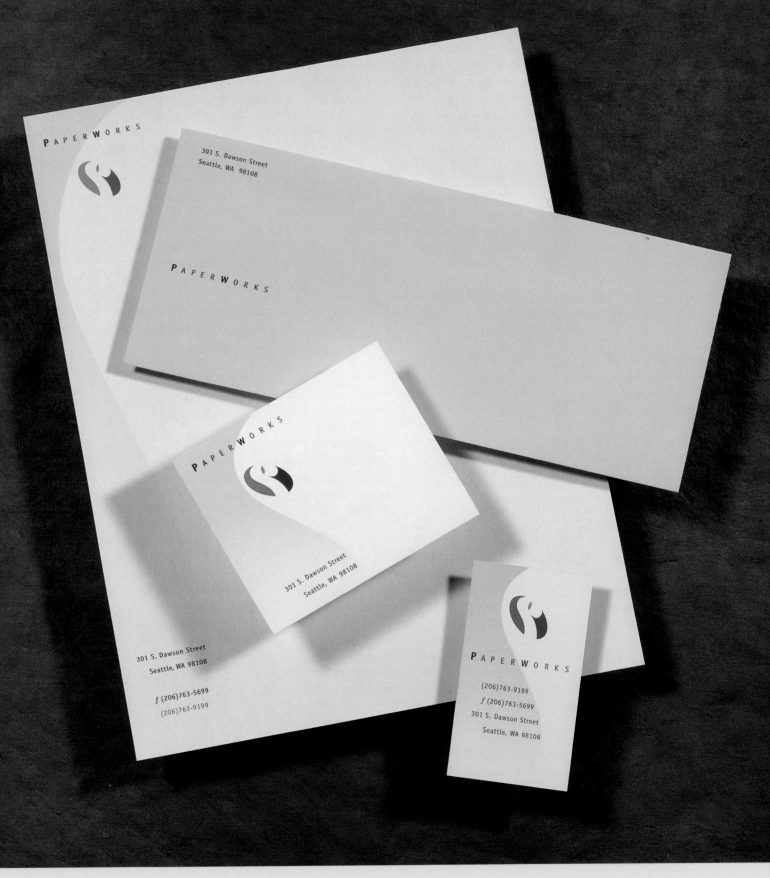

**DESIGN FIRM** | BELYEA DESIGN ALLIANCE

**ART DIRECTOR** | PATRICIA BELYEA

**DESIGNER** | CHRISTIAN SALAS

**CLIENT** | PAPERWORKS

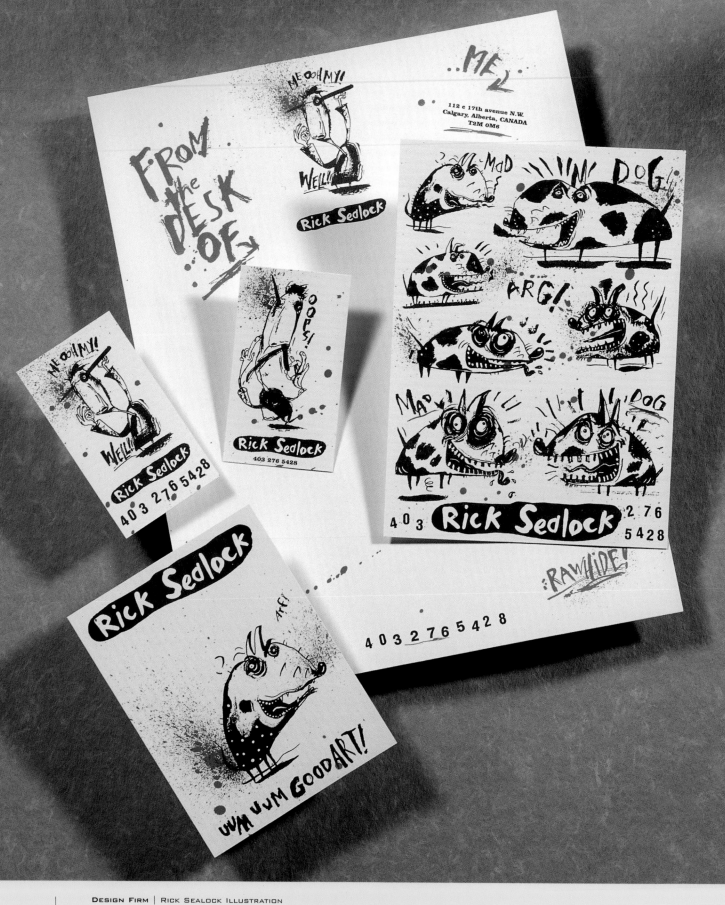

DESIGN FIRM | RICK SEALOCK ILLUSTRATION

ALL DESIGN | RICK SEALOCK

CLIENT | RICK SEALOCK

TOOLS | FOUND TYPE/PHOTOCOPIER

PAPER/PRINTING | CLASSIC COLUMN/OFFSET

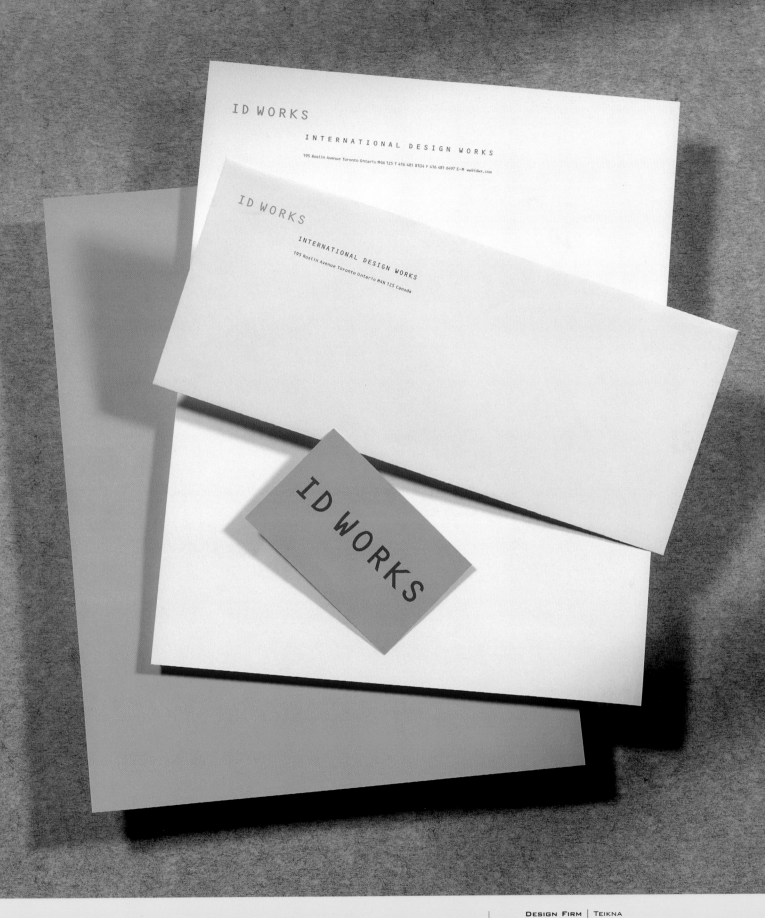

ID WORKS

INTERNATIONAL DESIGN WORKS

195 Roslin Avenue Toronto Ontario M4N 1Z5 T 416 481 8104 F 416 481 6497 E-M www.idwx.com

ID WORKS

INTERNATIONAL DESIGN WORKS

195 Roslin Avenue Toronto Ontario M4N 1Z5 Canada

ID WORKS

DESIGN FIRM | TEIKNA

ART DIRECTOR/DESIGNER | CLAUDIA NERI

CLIENT | ID WORKS

TOOLS | QUARKXPRESS

PAPER/PRINTING | MOHAWK OPTIONS/TWO COLOR

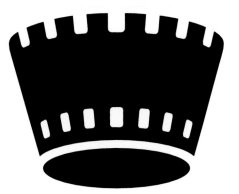

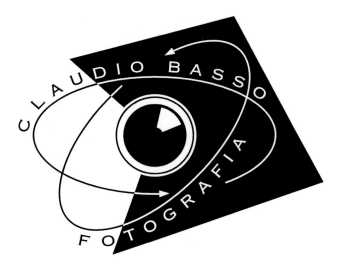

DESIGN FIRM | SIBLEY/PETEET DESIGN
DESIGNER | TOM KIRSCH
CLIENT | MIKE KING

DESIGN FIRM | VOSS DESIGN
ART DIRECTOR/DESIGNER | AXEL VOSS
CLIENT | CLAUDIO BASSO

MONKEY 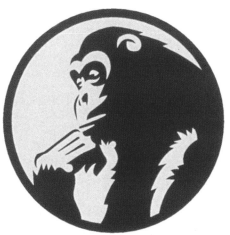 STUDIOS

DESIGN FIRM | TRACY SABIN GRAPHIC DESIGN
ART DIRECTOR | RUSSELL SABIN
ILLUSTRATOR | TRACY SABIN
CLIENT | MONKEY STUDIOS
TOOLS | ADOBE ILLUSTRATOR

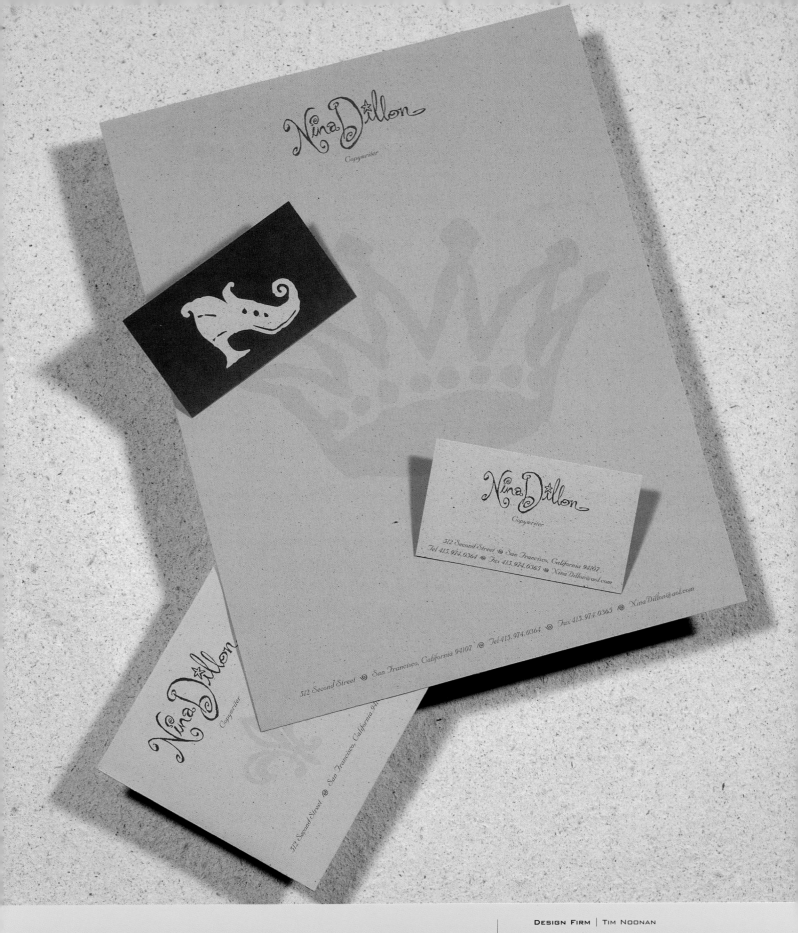

DESIGN FIRM | TIM NOONAN

DESIGNER | TIM NOONAN

CLIENT | NINA DILLON

TOOLS | QUARKXPRESS, HAND LETTERING

PAPER/PRINTING | SIMPSON QUEST/ONE PMS

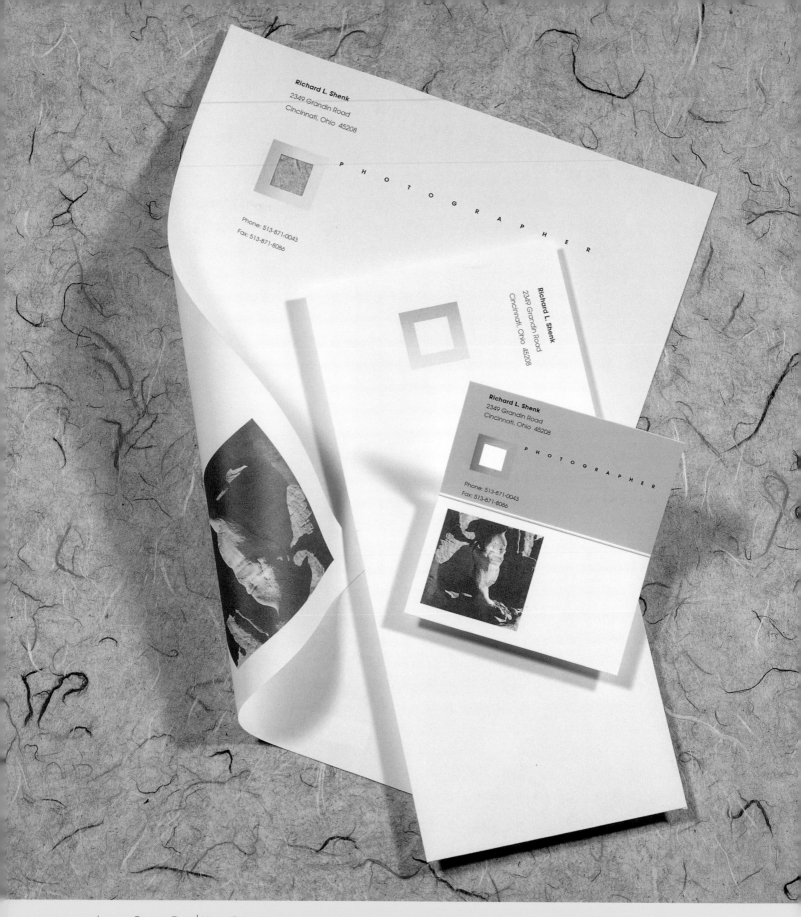

DESIGN FIRM | WOOD/BROD DESIGN
ALL DESIGN | STAN BROD
CLIENT | RICHARD L. SHENK
TOOLS | ADOBE ILLUSTRATOR

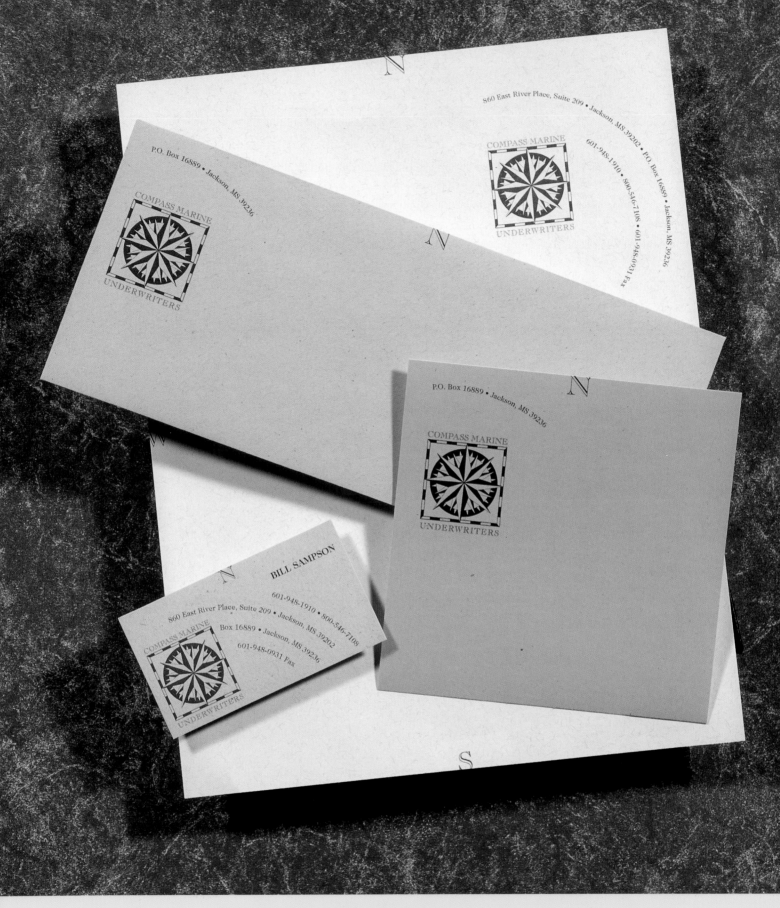

DESIGN FIRM | COMMUNICATION ARTS COMPANY

ART DIRECTOR | HAP OWEN

DESIGNER | ANNE-MARIE OTVOS

CLIENT | COMPASS MARINE UNDERWRITERS

TOOLS | MACINTOSH

PAPER/PRINTING | PROTERRA PARCHMENT &

STUCO, KRAFT/OFFSET LITHOGRAPHY

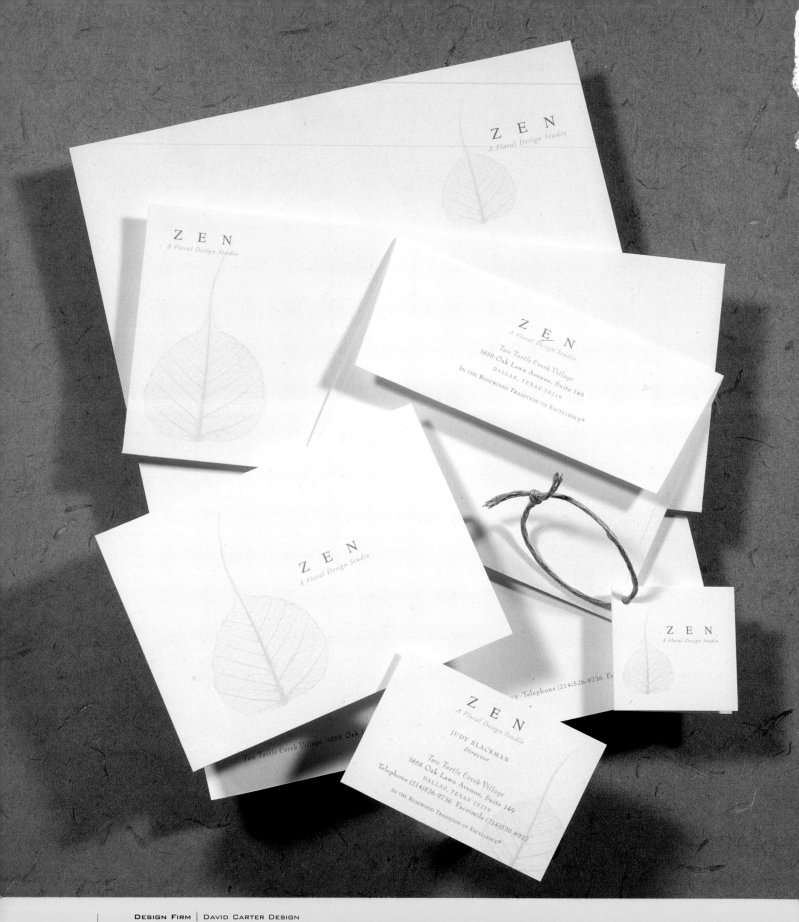

DESIGN FIRM | DAVID CARTER DESIGN
ART DIRECTORS | SHARON LeJEUNE, LORI B. WILSON
CLIENT | ZEN FLORAL DESIGN STUDIO
PAPER/PRINTING | SIMPSON EVERGREEN BIRCH/JARVIS PRESS

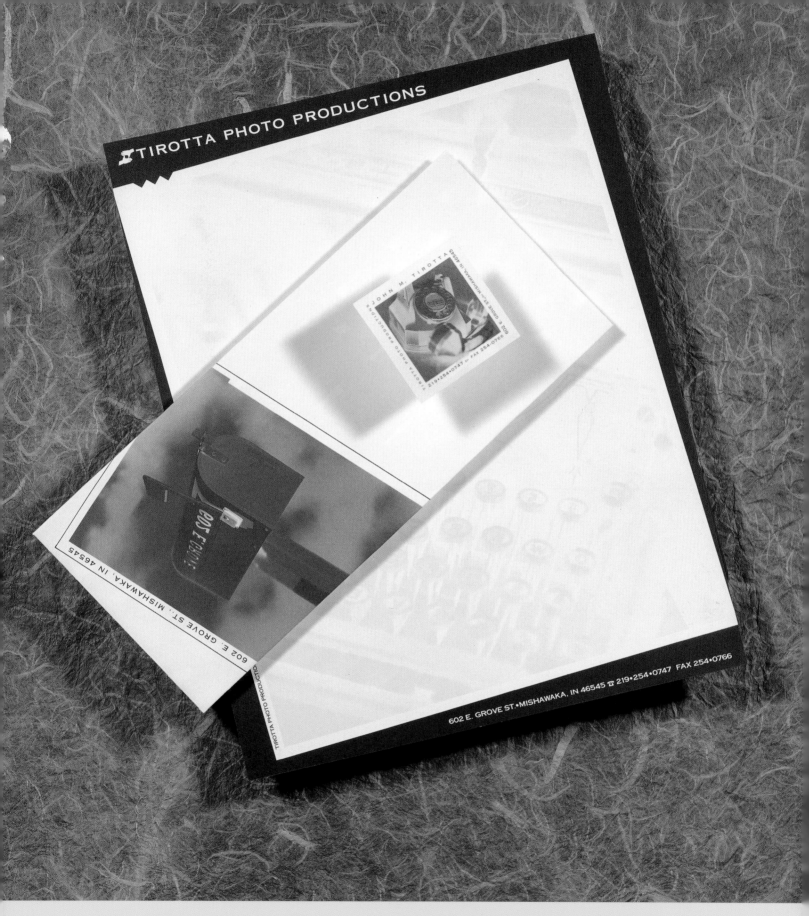

DESIGN FIRM | HIEROGLYPHICS ART & DESIGN
DESIGNER | CHRISTINE OSBORN TIROTTA
PHOTOGRAPHER | JOHN TIROTTA
CLIENT | TIROTTA PHOTO PRODUCTIONS
PAPER/PRINTING | STARWHITE VICKSBURG, UV ULTRA II

**Pesona Pictures Sdn Bhd**
159A Jalan Aminuddin Baki
Taman Tun Dr Ismail
60000 Kuala Lumpur *Malaysia*
*Tel* 603 719 1602 ✦ 718 2316
*Fax* 603 719 1586

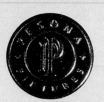

*Studio*
24 Jalan Kemajuan 12/18
46200 Petaling Jaya
Selangor Darul Ehsan *Malaysia*
*Tel* 603 754 2334 ✦ 754 2276
*Fax* 603 754 2335

**Pesona Pictures Sdn Bhd**
159A Jalan Aminuddin Baki
Taman Tun Dr Ismail
60000 Kuala Lumpur *Malaysia*
*Tel* 603 719 1602 ✦ 718 2316
*Fax* 603 719 1586

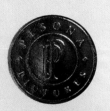

*Studio*
24 Jalan Kemajuan 12/18
46200 Petaling Jaya
Selangor Darul Ehsan *Malaysia*
*Tel* 603 754 2334 ✦ 754 2276
*Fax* 603 754 2335

DESIGN FIRM | WERK-HAUS
ART DIRECTOR | EZRAH RAHIM
DESIGNERS | ELRAH RAHIM, WAI MING, WEE
CLIENT | PESONA PICTURES
PAPER/PRINTING | CONCEPT WAVE SAND/ONE
    COLOR, COPPER HOT STAMPING, EMBOSSING

DESIGN FIRM | KIKU OBATA & COMPANY

ART DIRECTOR/DESIGNER | RICH NELSON

CLIENT | KIKU OBATA & COMPANY

PAPER/PRINTING | REPROX

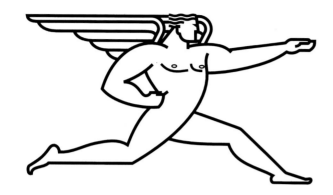

TOWER of BABEL

DESIGN FIRM | SIBLEY/PETEET DESIGN
DESIGNER | TOM HOUGH
CLIENT | MERCURY MESSENGER

DESIGN FIRM | TOWER OF BABEL
DESIGNER | ERIC STEVENS
CLIENT | TOWER OF BABEL

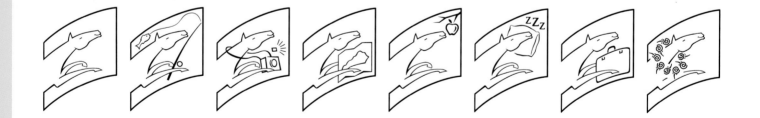

DESIGN FIRM | KIRBY STEPHENS DESIGN, INC.
ART DIRECTOR/DESIGNER | KIRBY STEPHENS
ILLUSTRATORS | DANIEL DUTTON, WILLIAM V. COX
CLIENT | KENTUCKY TOURISM COUNCIL
TOOLS | PENCIL, MACINTOSH PPC, SCANNER

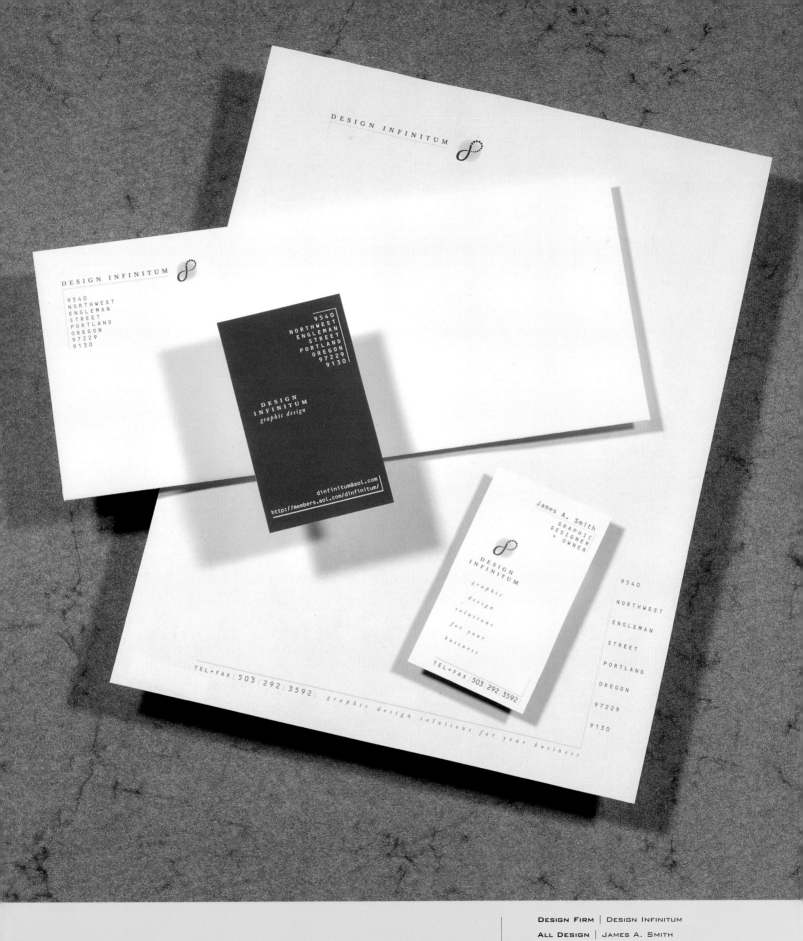

DESIGN FIRM | DESIGN INFINITUM

ALL DESIGN | JAMES A. SMITH

CLIENT | DESIGN INFINITUM

TOOLS | QUARKXPRESS, ADOBE ILLUSTRATOR

PAPER/PRINTING | BECKETT EXPRESSION/

CHROMAGRAPHICS

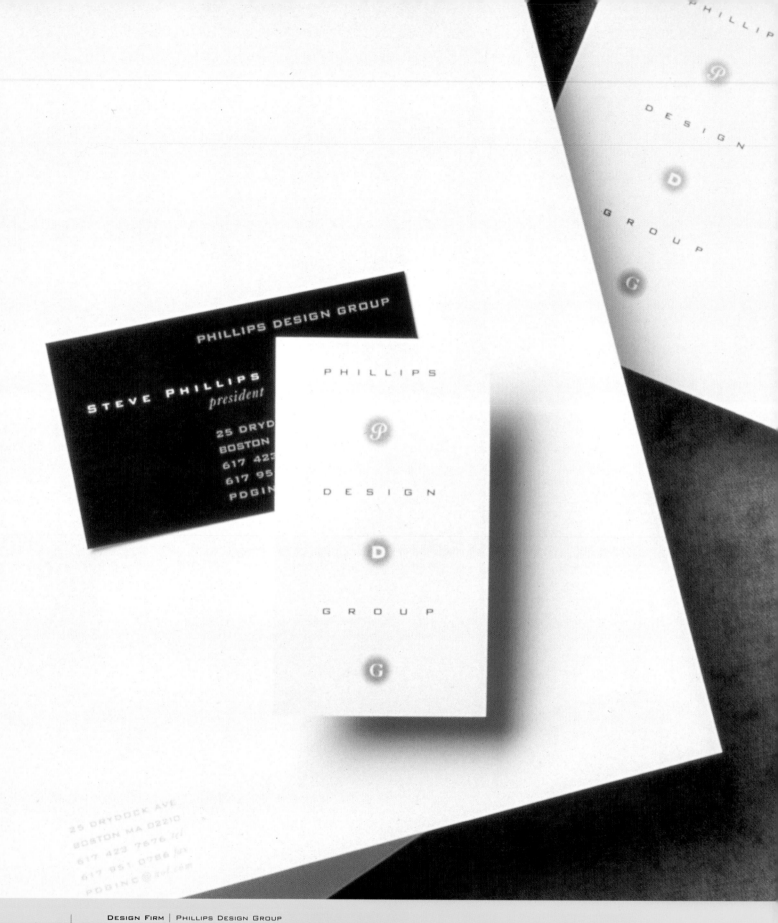

DESIGN FIRM | PHILLIPS DESIGN GROUP

ART DIRECTOR | STEVE PHILLIPS

DESIGNERS | BETH PARKER, ALISON GOUDREAULT

CLIENT | PHILLIPS DESIGN GROUP

TOOLS | ADOBE ILLUSTRATOR

PAPER/PRINTING | STRATHMORE/MARAN PRINTING

DESIGN FIRM | WEBSTER DESIGN ASSOCIATES

ART DIRECTOR | DAVE WEBSTER

DESIGNER/ILLUSTRATOR | ANDREY NAGORNY

CLIENT | DIE WORKS

TOOLS | MACROMEDIA FREEHAND

PAPER/PRINTING | CROSS POINTE GENESIS FOSSIL,
FOIL STAMPED

**AXIS**
*design corp*

*1 franklin avenue, rosemont, pennsylvania 19010-2705   fax: (610) 527-1095   phone: (610) 527-0332*

DESIGN FIRM | AXIS DESIGN

ART DIRECTOR/DESIGNER | WILLIAM MILNAZIK

CLIENT | AXIS DESIGN

PAPER/PRINTING | STRATHMORE ELEMENTS

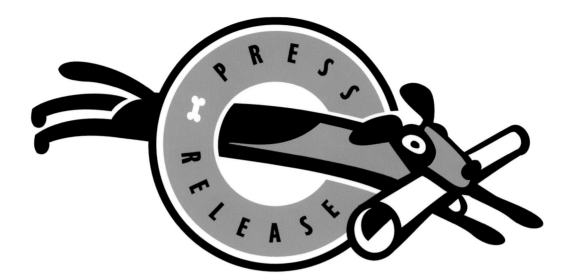

DESIGN FIRM | DOGSTAR
DESIGNER/ILLUSTRATOR | RODNEY DAVIDSON
CLIENT | DOGSTAR
TOOLS | ADOBE ILLUSTRATOR, STREAMLINE, MACROMEDIA FREEHAND

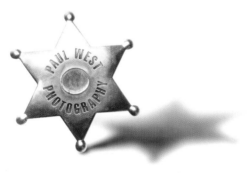

DESIGN FIRM | STORM DESIGN & ADVERTISING CONSULTANCY
ART DIRECTORS/DESIGNERS | DAVID ANSETT, DEAN BUTLER
ILLUSTRATORS | DEAN BUTLER, DAVID ANSETT
CLIENT | PAUL WEST PHOTOGRAPHY
TOOLS | ADOBE PHOTOSHOP

DESIGN FIRM | "SAY AH!" CREATIVE
ART DIRECTOR/DESIGNER | KELLY D. LAWRENCE
PHOTOGRAPHY | SUPERSTOCK
PRODUCTION | JON EMPEY, VICKIE MARTIN
CLIENT | "SAY AH!" CREATIVE
TOOLS | QUARKXPRESS, ADOBE PHOTOSHOP, ADOBE ILLUSTRATOR

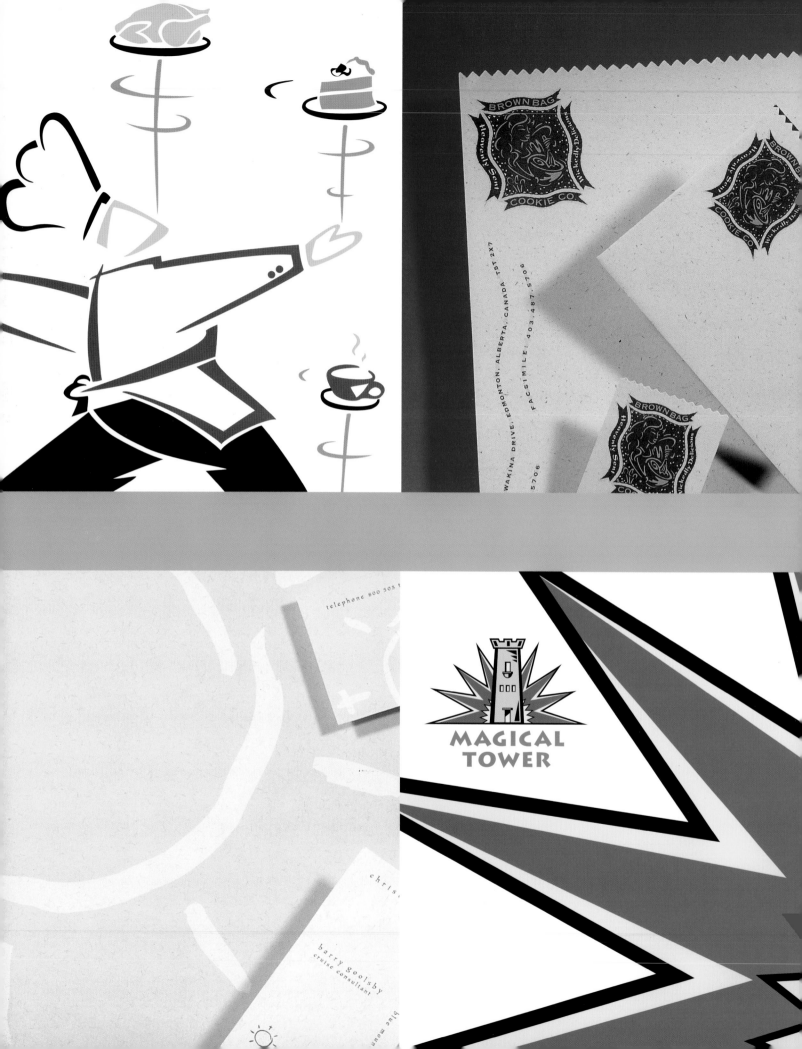

BROWN BAG
COOKIE CO.
Heavenly Sent · Wickedly Delicious

WAKINA DRIVE, EDMONTON, ALBERTA, CANADA T5T 2X7
FACSIMILE: 403.487.5706
5706

telephone 800 505

barry goolsby
cruise consultant

chris

MAGICAL
TOWER

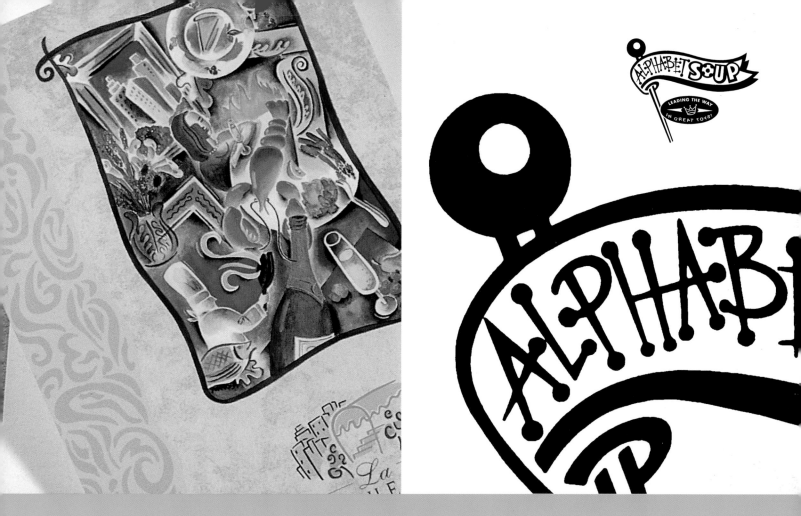

## RESTAURANT, RETAIL, AND HOSPITALITY

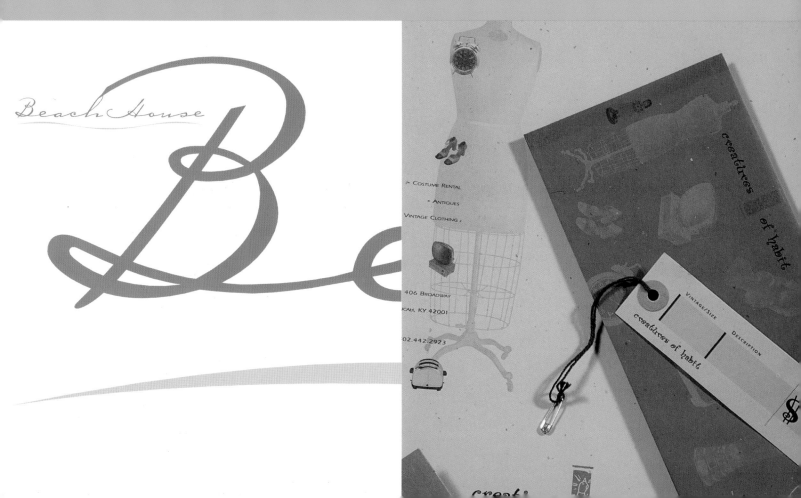

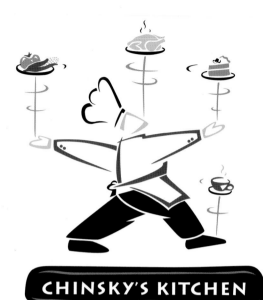

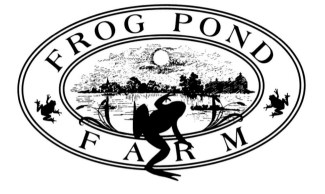

DESIGN FIRM | KIKU OBATA & COMPANY
ART DIRECTOR/DESIGNER  JOE FLORESCA
CLIENT | CHINSKY'S KITCHEN

DESIGN FIRM | TURNER DESIGN
ALL DESIGN | BERT TURNER
CLIENT | FROG POND FARM

# CASA de FRUTA

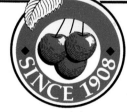

DESIGN FIRM | THARP DID IT
ART DIRECTOR | RICK THARP
DESIGNERS | RICK THARP, KIM TOMLINSON
CLIENT | CASA DE FRUTA
TOOLS | INK

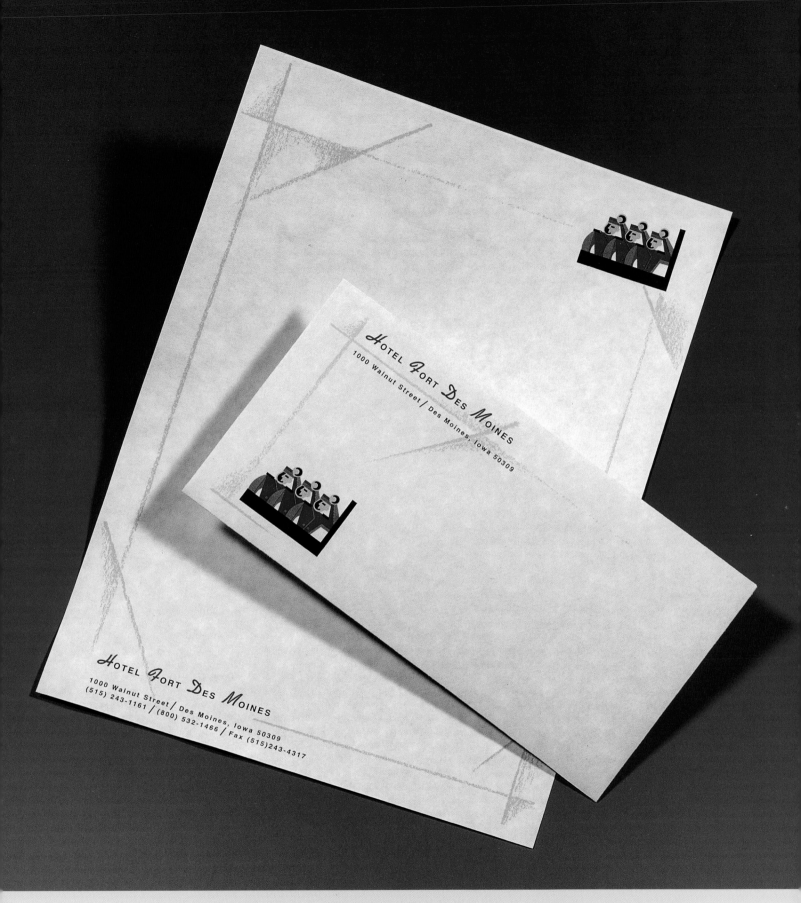

HOTEL FORT DES MOINES

1000 Walnut Street / Des Moines, Iowa 50309

HOTEL FORT DES MOINES

1000 Walnut Street / Des Moines, Iowa 50309
(515) 243-1161 / (800) 532-1466 / Fax (515)243-4317

DESIGN FIRM | SAYLES GRAPHIC DESIGN

ALL DESIGN | JOHN SAYLES

CLIENT | HOTEL FORT DES MOINES

PAPER/PRINTING | HOPPER SKYTONE NATURAL/OFFSET

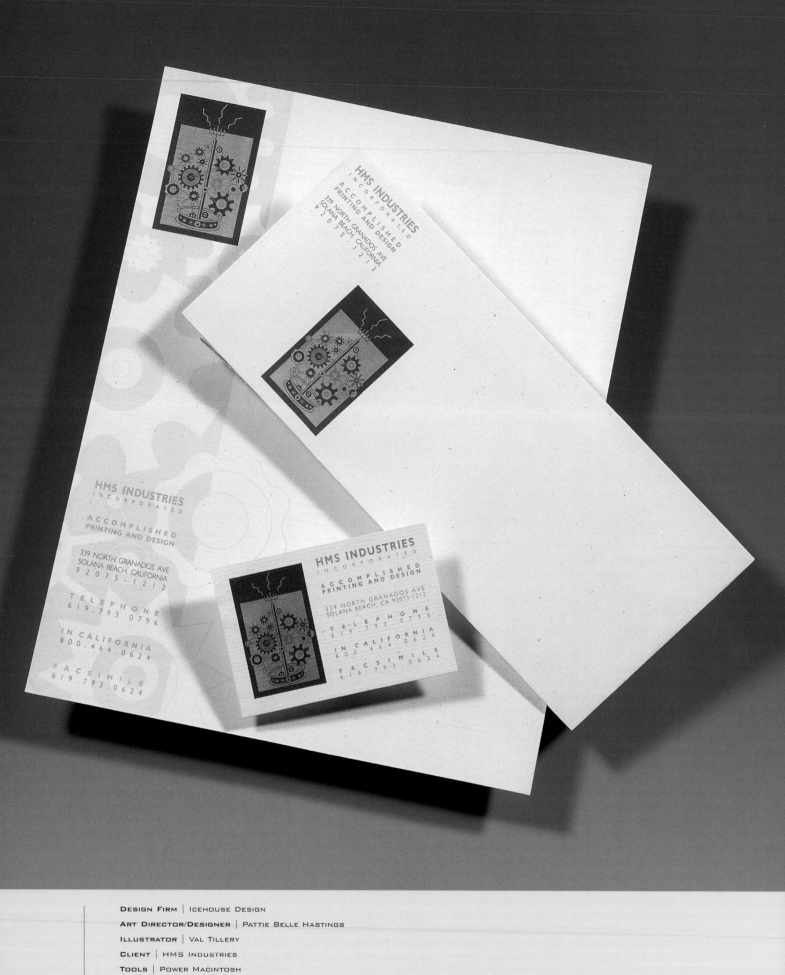

DESIGN FIRM | ICEHOUSE DESIGN
ART DIRECTOR/DESIGNER | PATTIE BELLE HASTINGS
ILLUSTRATOR | VAL TILLERY
CLIENT | HMS INDUSTRIES
TOOLS | POWER MACINTOSH
PAPER/PRINTING | CLASSIC CREST

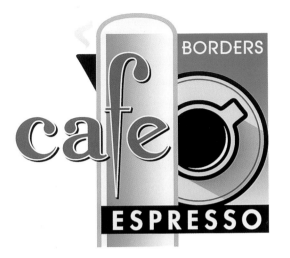

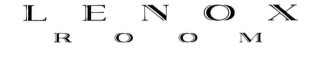

TIP WELL AND PROSPER

DESIGN FIRM | FRCH Design Worldwide
ART DIRECTOR | Joan Donnelly
DESIGNER/ILLUSTRATOR | Tim A. Frame
CLIENT | Borders Books and Music
TOOLS | Adobe Illustrator

DESIGN FIRM | Aerial
ART DIRECTOR/DESIGNER | Tracy Moon
PHOTOGRAPHY | R. J. Muna
CLIENT | Lenox Room Restaurant
TOOLS | Adobe Photoshop, QuarkXPress

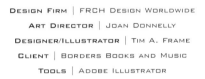

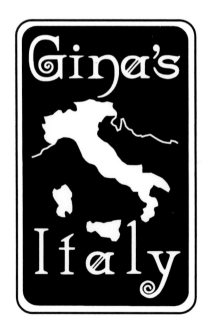

DESIGN FIRM | Flaherty Art & Design
ALL DESIGN | Marie Flaherty
CLIENT | The O Bar of Eating Up the Coast
TOOLS | Adobe Illustrator

DESIGN FIRM | Jeff Fisher Logomotives
ALL DESIGN | Jeff Fisher
CLIENT | Triad (ad agency for Gina's Italy)
TOOLS | Macromedia FreeHand

# MONSOON CAFE

DESIGN FIRM | VRONTIKIS DESIGN OFFICE

ART DIRECTOR | PETRULA VRONTIKIS

DESIGNER | LISA CRITCHFIELD

CLIENT | HASEGAWA ENTERPRISES

TOOLS | QUARKXPRESS, ADOBE PHOTOSHOP

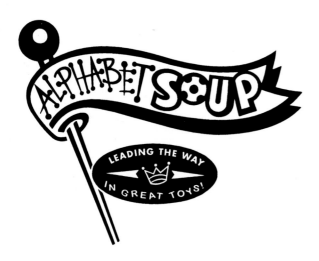

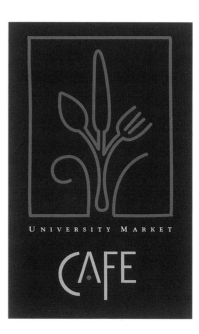

DESIGN FIRM | SAYLES GRAPHIC DESIGN

ALL DESIGN | JOHN SAYLES

CLIENT | ALPHABET SOUP

DESIGN FIRM | CORNOYER-HEDRICK, INC.

ART DIRECTOR | JIM BOLEK

DESIGNER/ILLUSTRATOR | LANIE GOTCHER

CLIENT | MOTOROLA

TOOLS | ADOBE ILLUSTRATOR

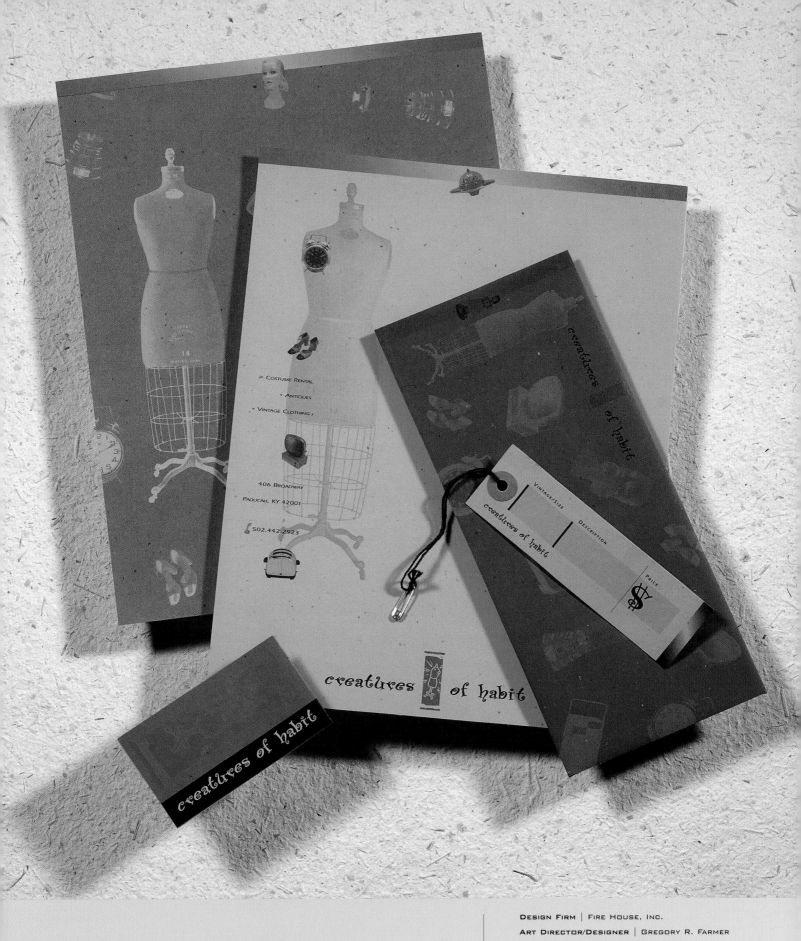

DESIGN FIRM │ FIRE HOUSE, INC.

ART DIRECTOR/DESIGNER │ GREGORY R. FARMER

CLIENT │ CREATURES OF HABIT

TOOLS │ QUARKXPRESS, ADOBE PHOTOSHOP

PAPER/PRINTING │ FOX RIVER CONFETTI, MOORE-LANGEN

PRINTING COMPANY, KENNY GRAPHICS

DESIGN FIRM | THE PROVEN EDGE

ALL DESIGN | RITA GOLD

CLIENT | NATURAL INDULGENCE

TOOLS | ADOBE ILLUSTRATOR

PAPER/PRINTING | CROSS POINTE/FRASER AND HOPPER, PRIORITY

PRINTERS AND EPSON STYLUS PRO WITH BINARY POWER RIP

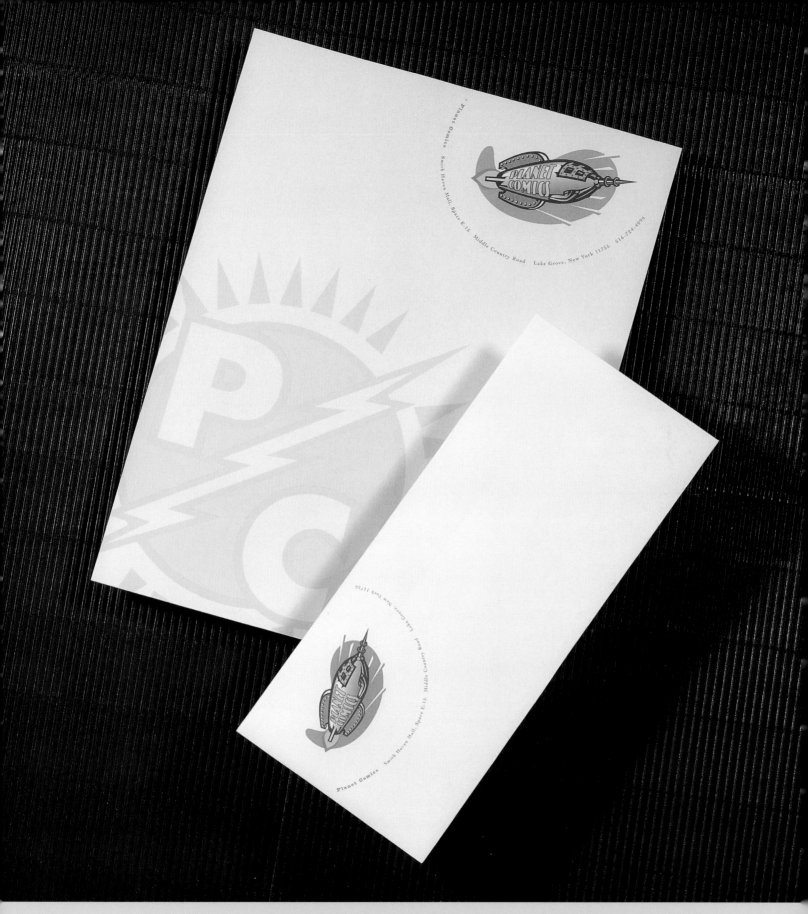

DESIGN FIRM | KIKU OBATA & COMPANY
ART DIRECTOR/DESIGNER | RICH NELSON
CLIENT | PLANET COMICS

Natural Indulgence

6856 cibola road, san diego, ca 92120 usa

Natural Indulgence

...the experience you were meant for

amal h. bernal, m.s.
president & ceo
6856 cibola road
san diego, ca 92120 usa
tel 1 619 287 4514 & fax 1 619 265 1211

Natural Indulgence

6856 cibola road, san diego, ca 92120 usa     tel 1 619 287 4514 & fax 1 619 265 1211

Indulge in the power of natural beauty. It is the experience you were meant for.

DESIGN FIRM | THE PROVEN EDGE

ALL DESIGN | RITA GOLD

CLIENT | NATURAL INDULGENCE

TOOLS | ADOBE ILLUSTRATOR

PAPER/PRINTING | CROSS POINTE/FRASER AND HOPPER, PRIORITY

PRINTERS AND EPSON STYLUS PRO WITH BINARY POWER RIP

DESIGN FIRM | ON THE EDGE
ART DIRECTOR | JEFF GASPER
DESIGNER | GINA MIMS
ILLUSTRATOR | RUSS MIMS
CLIENT | PLAYERS SPORTS GRILL
TOOLS | QUARKXPRESS, ADOBE ILLUSTRATOR, ADOBE PHOTOSHOP
PAPER/PRINTING | EVERGREEN WHITE

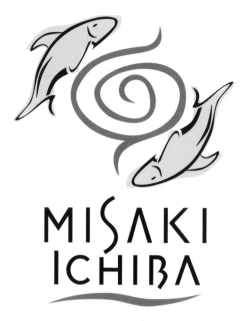

# MISAKI ICHIBA

DESIGN FIRM | KIKU OBATA & COMPANY
ART DIRECTOR | JOE FLORESCA
DESIGNERS | JOE FLORESCA, JEFF RIFKIN, ELEANOR SAFE
CLIENT | R.I.C. DESIGN

dog lips

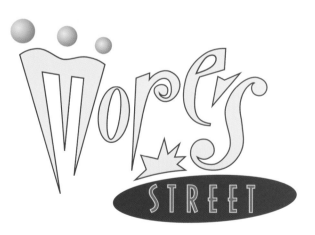

DESIGN FIRM | JUICE DESIGN
ART DIRECTOR/DESIGNER | BRETT M. CRITCHCHLOW
CLIENT | DOGLIPS

DESIGN FIRM | KIKU OBATA & COMPANY
ART DIRECTOR/DESIGNER | RICH NELSON
CLIENT | R.I.C. DESIGN

DESIGN FIRM | ON THE EDGE

ART DIRECTOR | JEFF GASPER

DESIGNER | GINA MIMS

ILLUSTRATOR | ERIC PETERSON

CLIENT | JT SCHMID'S BREWHOUSE & EATERY

TOOLS | ADOBE ILLUSTRATOR, QUARKXPRESS

PAPER/PRINTING | CLASSIC CREST IVORY CARD,

LUNA WHITE COVER/FIVE COLOR

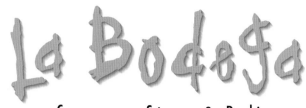

Company Store & Deli

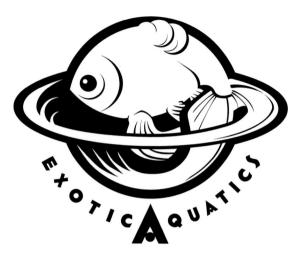

DESIGN FIRM | FLAHERTY ART & DESIGN

ALL DESIGN | MARIE FLAHERTY

CLIENT | LA BODEGA OF EATING UP THE COAST

TOOLS | ADOBE ILLUSTRATOR

DESIGN FIRM | S&N DESIGN

ALL DESIGN | CRAIG GOODMAN

CLIENT | EXOTIC AQUATICS

TOOLS | ADOBE ILLUSTRATOR

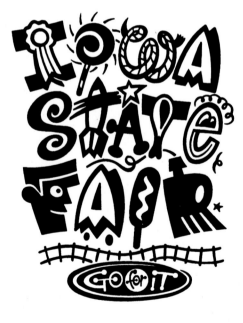

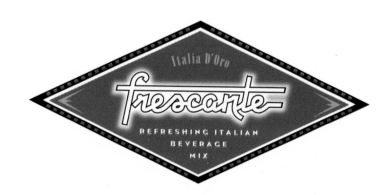

DESIGN FIRM | SAYLES GRAPHIC DESIGN

ART DIRECTOR/ILLUSTRATOR | JOHN SAYLES

DESIGNER | JOHN SAYLES, JENNIFER ELLIOTT

CLIENT | IOWA STATE FAIR

DESIGN FIRM | MIRES DESIGN

ART DIRECTORS | SCOTT MIRES, MIKE BROWER

DESIGNERS | MIKE BROWER, SCOTT MIRES

ILLUSTRATOR | TRACY SABIN

COPYWRITER | JOHN KURAOKA

CLIENT | FOOD GROUP/BOYDS COFFEE

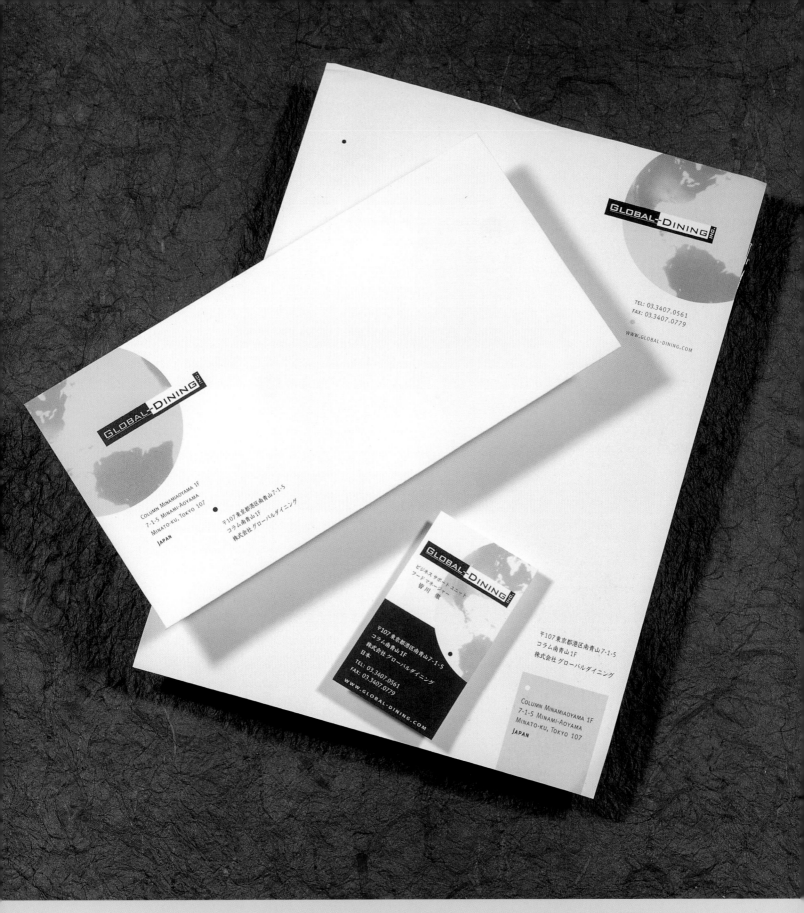

DESIGN FIRM | VRONTIKIS DESIGN OFFICE
ART DIRECTOR/DESIGNER | PETRULA VRONTIKIS
CLIENT | GLOBAL-DINING, INC.
TOOLS | QUARKXPRESS, ADOBE PHOTOSHOP
PAPER/PRINTING | NEENAH CLASSIC
CREST/DONAHUE PRINTING

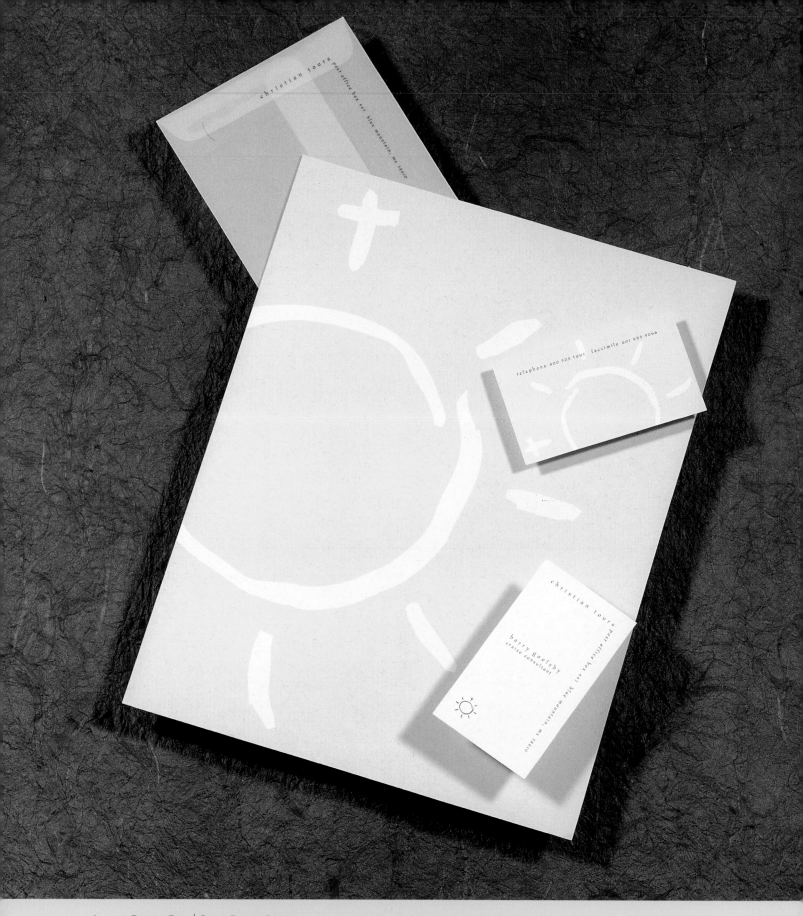

DESIGN FIRM | DAVID CARTER DESIGN

ART DIRECTOR | LORI B. WILSON, GARY LOBUE, JR.

DESIGNER/ILLUSTRATOR | TRACY HUCK

CLIENT | CHRISTIAN TOURS

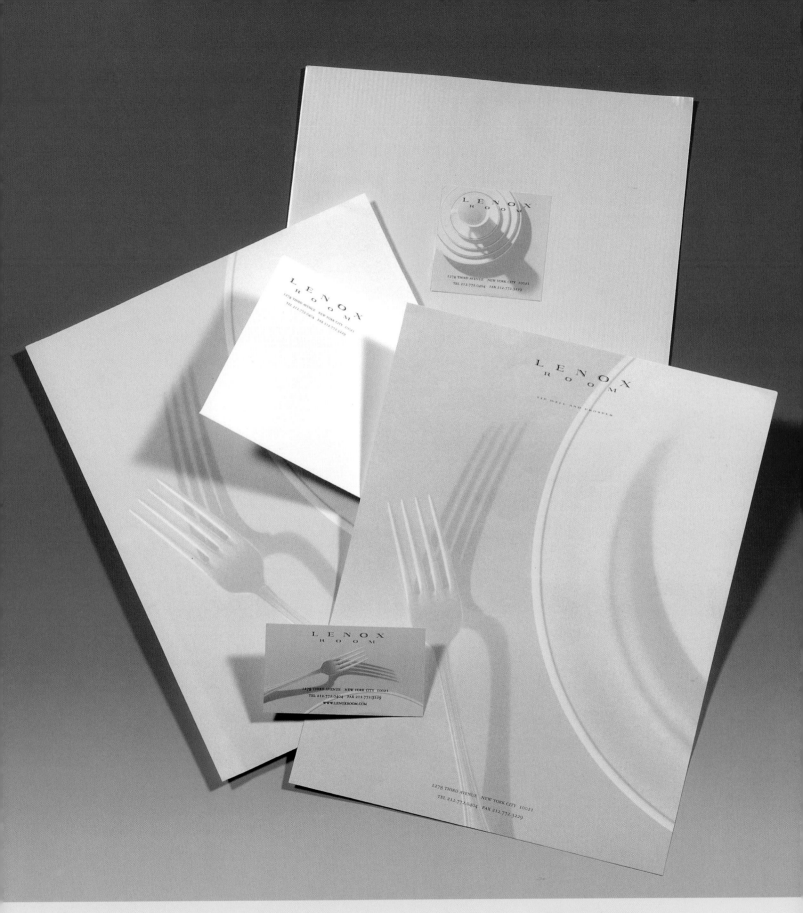

DESIGN FIRM | AERIAL

ART DIRECTOR/DESIGNER | TRACY MOON

PHOTOGRAPHY | R. J. MUNA

CLIENT | LENOX ROOM RESTAURANT

TOOLS | ADOBE PHOTOSHOP, QUARKXPRESS

PAPER/PRINTING | 24 LB. EVERGREEN IVORY

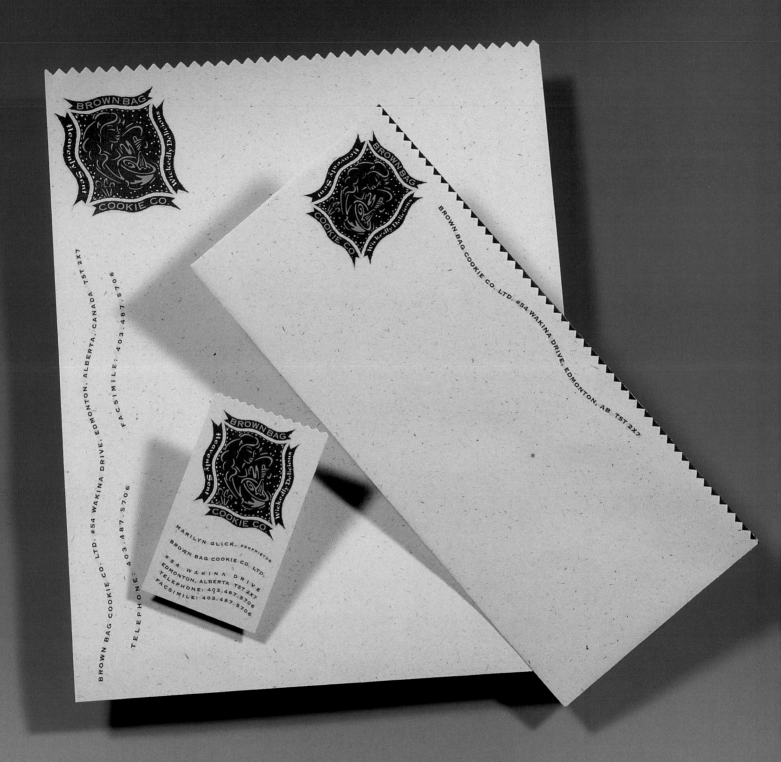

**DESIGN FIRM** | DUCK SOUP GRAPHICS

**ALL DESIGN** | WILLIAM DOUCETTE

**CLIENT** | BROWN BAG COOKIE COMPANY

**TOOLS** | ADOBE ILLUSTRATOR, QUARKXPRESS

**PAPER/PRINTING** | FRENCH SPECKLETONE/2 MATCH COLORS

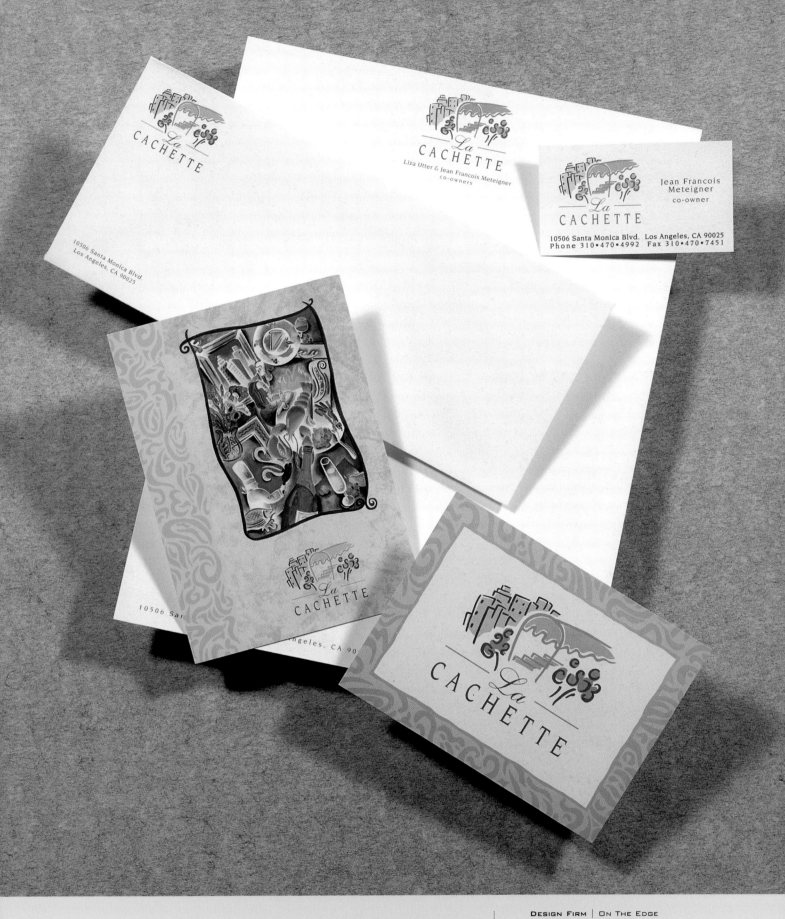

DESIGN FIRM | ON THE EDGE

ART DIRECTOR | JEFF GASPER

DESIGNER | GINA MIMS

ILLUSTRATOR | JEFF GASPER

CLIENT | LA CACHETTE

TOOLS | QUARKXPRESS, ADOBE ILLUSTRATOR,
ADOBE PHOTOSHOP

**GLOBAL-DINING INC.**

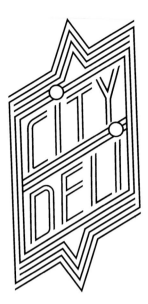

DESIGN FIRM | VRONTIKIS DESIGN OFFICE
ART DIRECTOR/DESIGNER | PETRULA VRONTIKIS
CLIENT | GLOBAL-DINING, INC.
TOOLS | QUARKXPRESS, ADOBE PHOTOSHOP
PAPER/PRINTING | NEENAH CLASSIC CREST/DONAHUE PRINTING

DESIGN FIRM | SOMMESE DESIGN
ART DIRECTOR/ILLUSTRATOR | LANNY SOMMESE
DESIGNER | LANNY SOMMESE, DEVIN PEDSWATER
CLIENT | PENNSYLVANIA STATE UNIVERSITY
TOOLS | ADOBE ILLUSTRATOR

*Beach House*

DESIGN FIRM | AERIAL
ART DIRECTOR/DESIGNER | TRACY MOON
CLIENT | BEACH HOUSE HOTEL
TOOLS | ADOBE ILLUSTRATOR
PAPER/PRINTING | LEEWOOD PRESS/SF

REBECCA'S
**MIGHTY**
MUFFINS

REBECCA'S
**MIGHTY**
MUFFINS

**BAKERY • DELI CAFE
ESPRESSO BAR**
514-A FRONT STREET
SANTA CRUZ, CA 95060
PHONE: 408-429-1940

DESIGN FIRM | FAIA DESIGN

ALL DESIGN | DON FAIA

CLIENT | REBECCA'S MIGHTY MUFFINS

TOOLS | ADOBE ILLUSTRATOR

PAPER/PRINTING | PROTOCOL WRITING/OFFSET

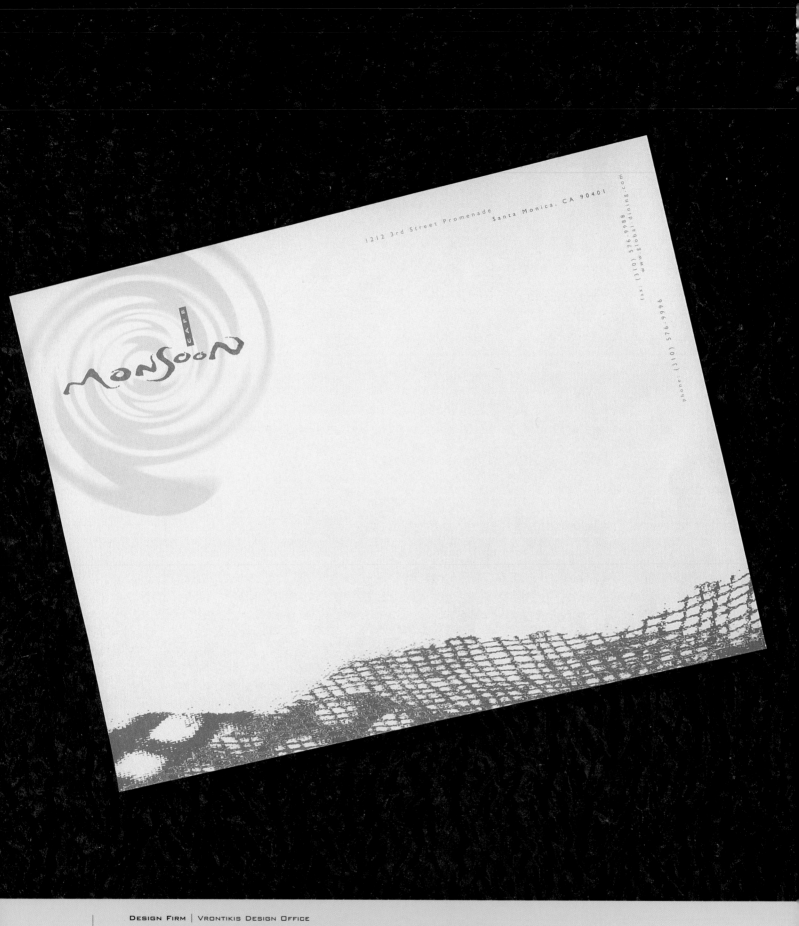

1212 3rd Street Promenade    Santa Monica, CA 90401

phone (310) 576-9996    fax (310) 576-9988    globalpidel@aol.com    www.ipdining.com

DESIGN FIRM │ VRONTIKIS DESIGN OFFICE

ART DIRECTOR │ PETRULA VRONTIKIS

DESIGNER │ LISA CRITCHFIELD

CLIENT │ HASEGAWA ENTERPRISES

TOOLS │ QUARKXPRESS, ADOBE PHOTOSHOP

PAPER/PRINTING │ CROSSPOINTE SYNERGY/LOGIN PRINTING

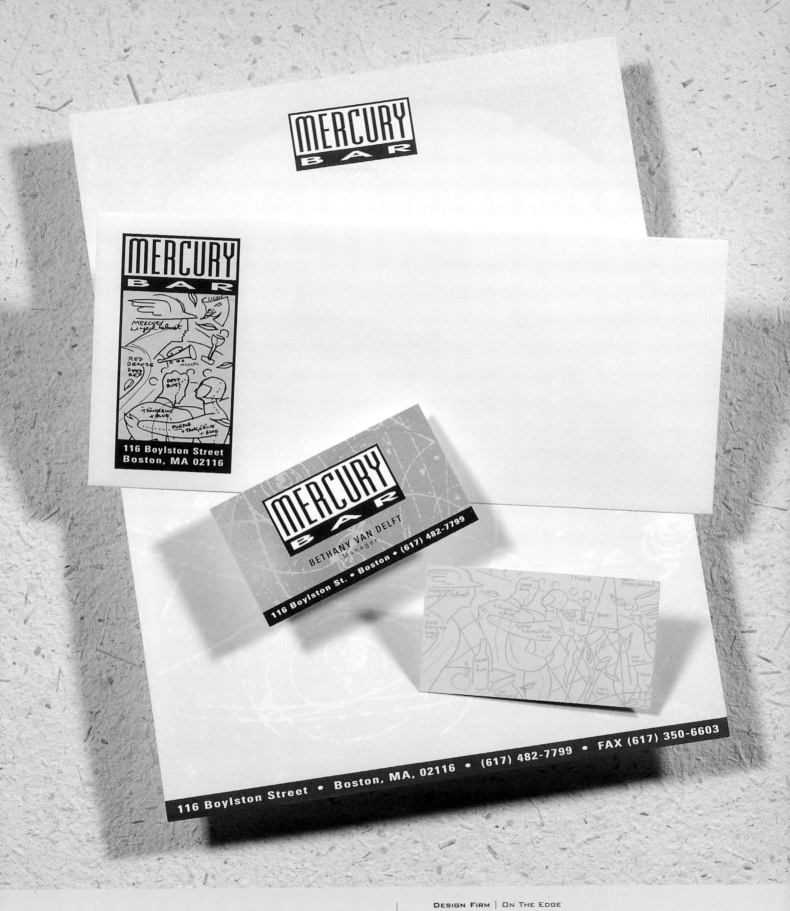

DESIGN FIRM | ON THE EDGE
ART DIRECTOR | JEFF GASPER
DESIGNER | GINA MIMS
ILLUSTRATOR | ANN FIELD
CLIENT | MERCURY BAR
TOOLS | ADOBE PHOTOSHOP, QUARKXPRESS, ADOBE ILLUSTRATOR
PAPER/PRINTING | CLASSIC CREST WHITE, LUNA WHITE COVER/FOUR COLOR

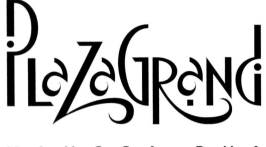

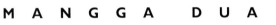

MANGGA DUA

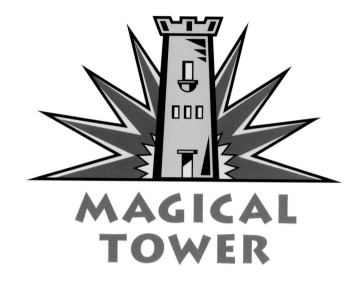

DESIGN FIRM | THAT'S CADIZ! ORIGINALS
ART DIRECTOR/DESIGNER | MINELEO CADIZ
CLIENT | PT MANGGA DUA TOWER
TOOLS | MACROMEDIA FREEHAND

DESIGN FIRM | KIKU OBATA & COMPANY
ART DIRECTOR | JOE FLORESCA
DESIGNERS | JOE FLORESCA, JEFF RIFKIN
CLIENT | R.I.C. DESIGN

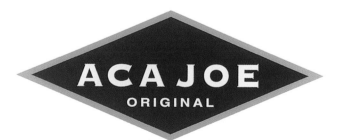

DESIGN FIRM | FRCH DESIGN WORLD WIDE
ART DIRECTOR | JOAN DONNELLY
DESIGNER | TIM A. FRAME
CLIENT | ACA JOE
TOOLS | ADOBE ILLUSTRATOR

DESIGN FIRM | TONI SCHOWALTER DESIGN
ALL DESIGN | TONI SCHOWALTER
CLIENT | WOMEN CHEFS & RESTAURATEURS
TOOLS | QUARKXPRESS, ADOBE ILLUSTRATOR

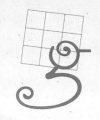

greenscreen

greenscreen

**AT:** atmospherics

1743 S. LA CIENEGA BLVD.

LOS ANGELES, CA

90035-4650

F - 310.837.0523

T - 800.450.3494

**AT:** atmospherics

DESIGN FIRM | CLIFFORD SELBERT DESIGN COLLABORATIVE

ART DIRECTOR | ROBIN PERKINS

DESIGNER | ROBIN PERKINS, HEATHER WATSON

CLIENT | ATMOSPHERICS

TOOLS | ADOBE ILLUSTRATOR

PAPER/PRINTING | GENESIS CROSS POINT 80 LB. TEXT/CHALLENGE GRAPHICS

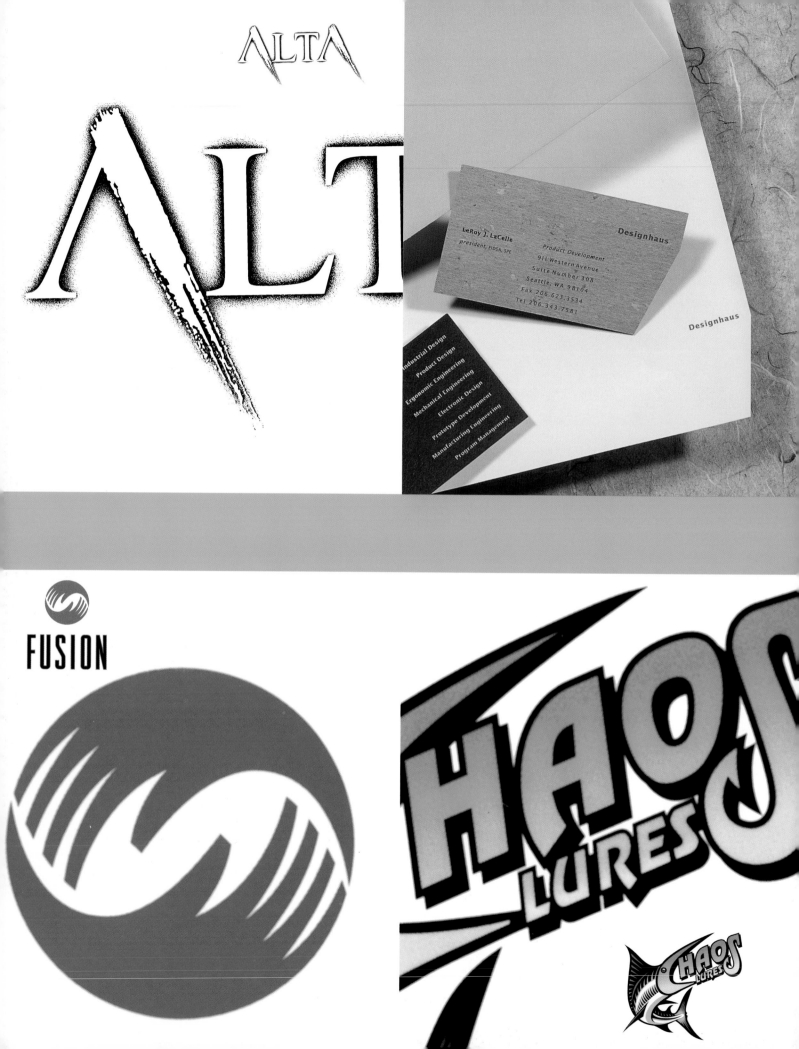

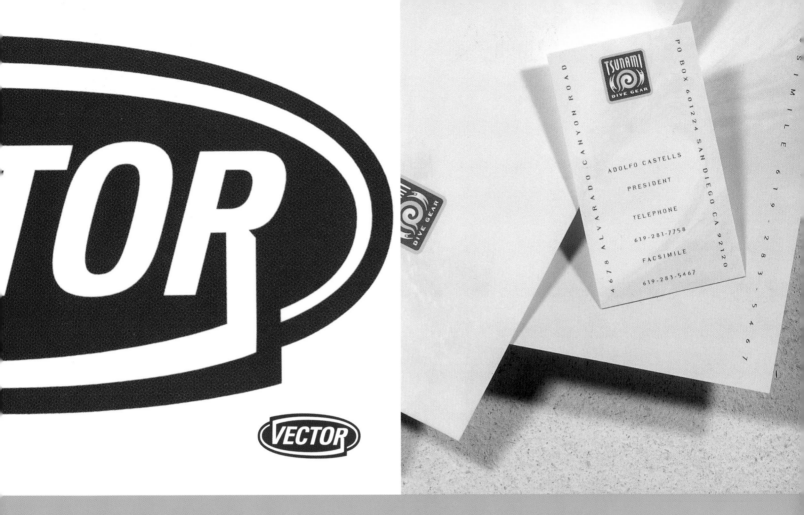

# INDUSTRY AND MANUFACTURE

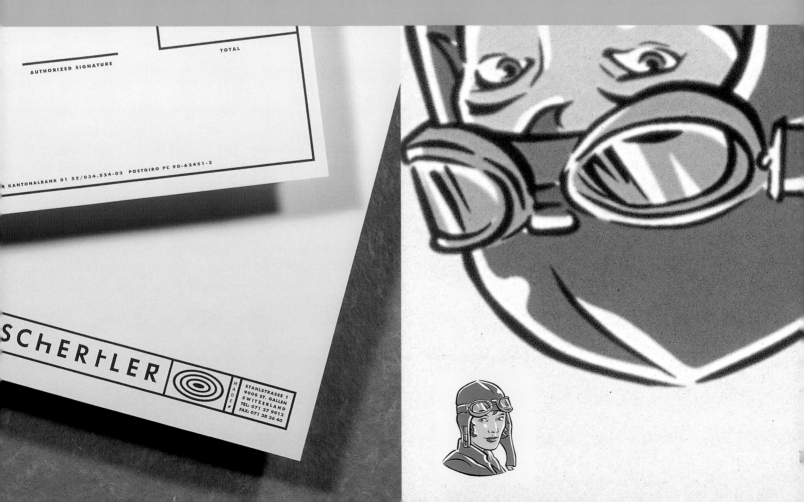

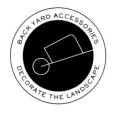

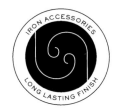

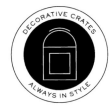

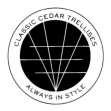

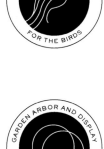

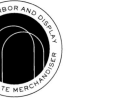

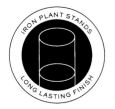

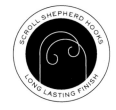

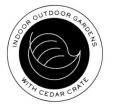

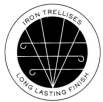

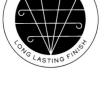

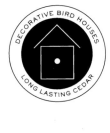

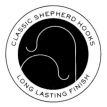

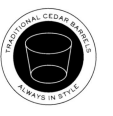

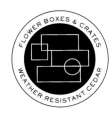

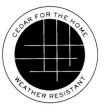

DESIGN FIRM | INSIGHT DESIGN COMMUNICATIONS

ALL DESIGN | SHERRIE AND TRACY HOLDEMAN

CLIENT | THE HAYES COMPANY

TOOLS | POWER MACINTOSH, MACROMEDIA FREEHAND

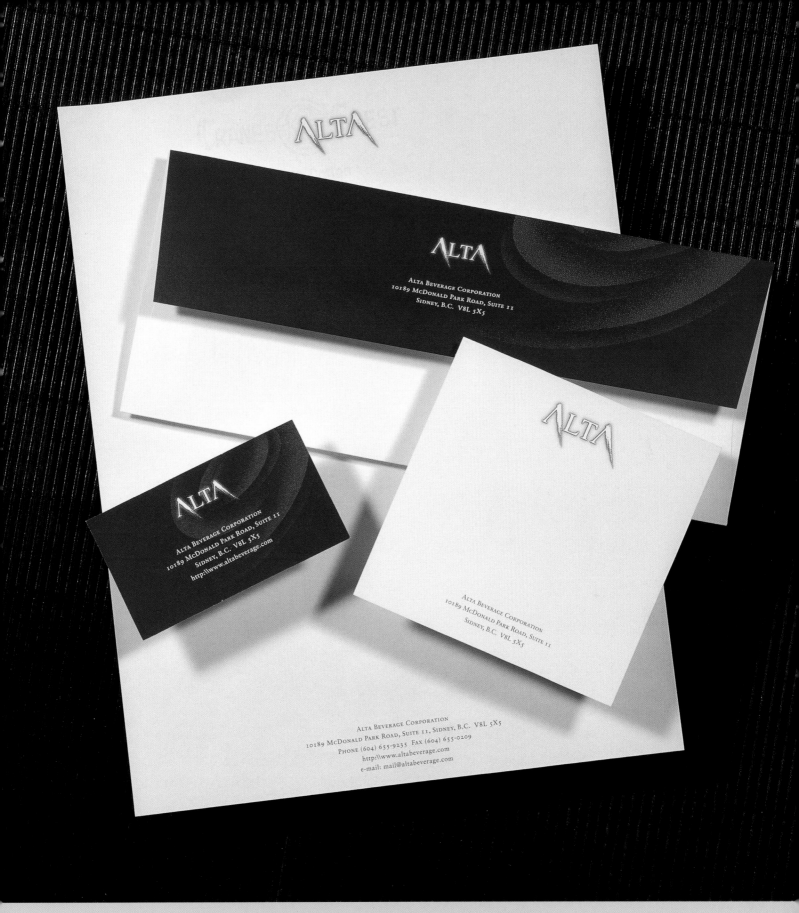

DESIGN FIRM | HORNALL ANDERSON DESIGN WORKS, INC.

ART DIRECTOR | JACK ANDERSON

DESIGNERS | JACK ANDERSON, LARRY ANDERSON,
JULIE KEENAN

CLIENT | ALTA BEVERAGE COMPANY

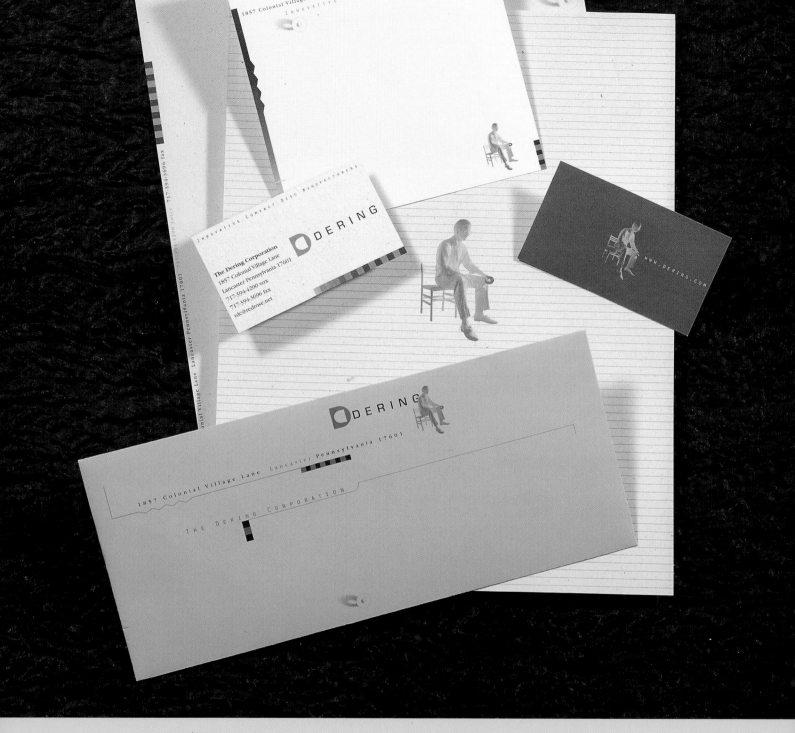

DESIGN FIRM | MUSSER DESIGN
ART DIRECTOR/DESIGNER | JERRY KING MUSSER
CLIENT | THE DERING CORPORATION
TOOLS | MACINTOSH, ADOBE ILLUSTRATOR

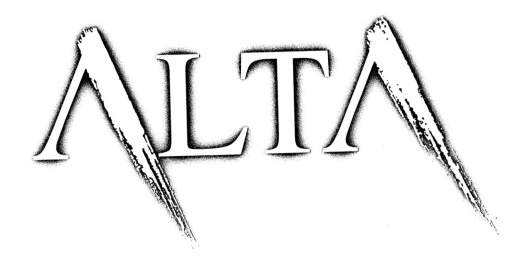

**DESIGN FIRM** | HORNALL ANDERSON DESIGN WORKS, INC.

**ART DIRECTOR** | JACK ANDERSON

**DESIGNERS** | JACK ANDERSON, LARRY ANDERSON, JULIE KEENAN

**CLIENT** | ALTA BEVERAGE COMPANY

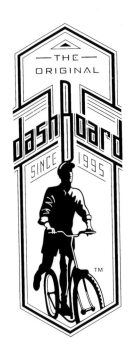

# Virtual Garden

**DESIGN FIRM** | THARP DID IT

**ART DIRECTOR** | RICK THARP

**DESIGNERS** | RICK THARP, NICOLE COLEMAN

**CLIENT** | TIME WARNER

**TOOLS** | MACINTOSH

**DESIGN FIRM** | THARP DID IT

**ART DIRECTORS** | RICK THARP, CHARLES DRUMMOND

**DESIGNER** | RICK THARP

**ILLUSTRATOR** | NICOLE COLEMAN

**CLIENT** | THE DASHBOARD COMPANY

**TOOLS** | INK, MACINTOSH

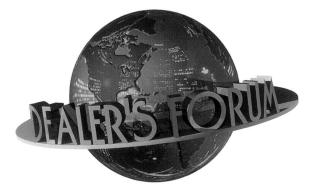

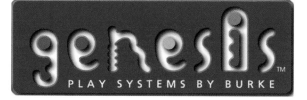

DESIGN FIRM | TRACY SABIN GRAPHIC DESIGN
ART DIRECTOR | RITA HOFFMAN
ILLUSTRATOR | TRACY SABIN
CLIENT | TAYLOR GUITARS
TOOLS | STRATA STUDIO PRO
PAPER/PRINTING | NEWSLETTER MEAD

DESIGN FIRM | HANSON/DODGE DESIGN
ART DIRECTOR | KEN HANSON
DESIGNER/ILLUSTRATOR | JACK HARGREAVES
CLIENT | BCI BURKE COMPANY
TOOLS | ADOBE ILLUSTRATOR, ADOBE PHOTOSHOP
PAPER/PRINTING | 60 LB. COATED TEXT/FOUR PROCESS COLORS

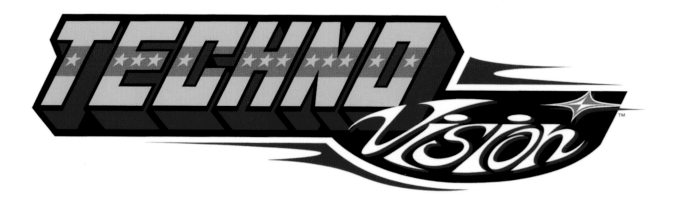

DESIGN FIRM | HANSON/DODGE DESIGN
ART DIRECTOR | LAURA SAMUELS
DESIGNER/ILLUSTRATOR | JACK HARGREAVES
CLIENT | TREK BICYCLE CORPORATION
TOOLS | ADOBE ILLUSTRATOR
PAPER/PRINTING | FOUR PROCESS COLORS PLUS GLOSS VARNISH, TEN POINT CIS

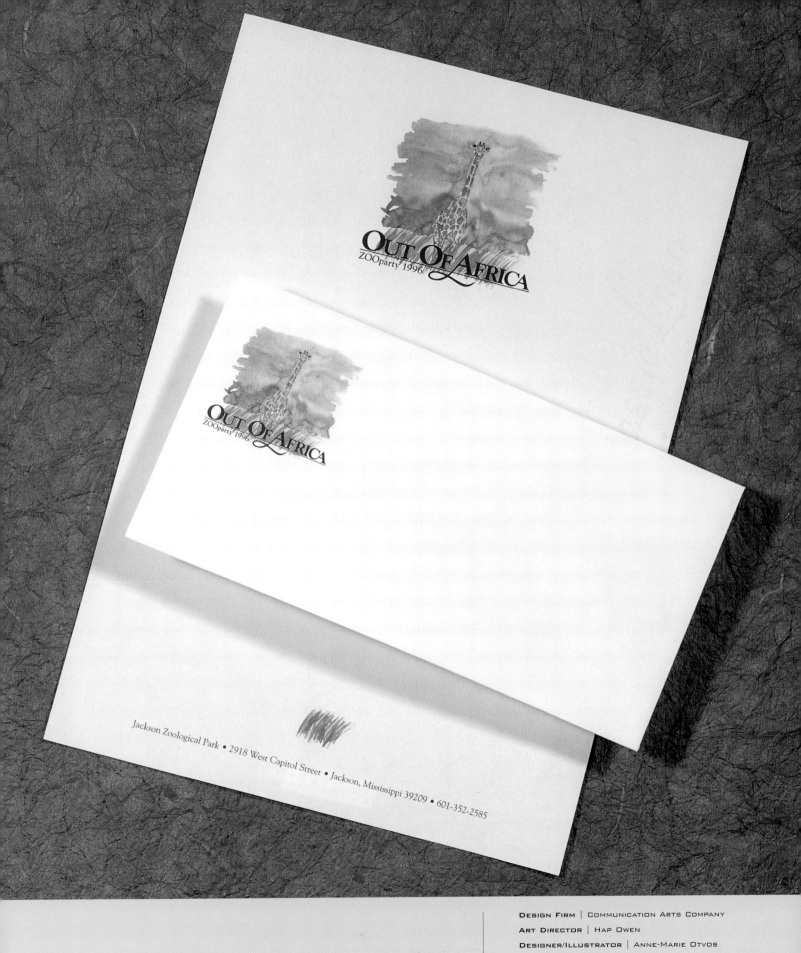

**DESIGN FIRM** | COMMUNICATION ARTS COMPANY

**ART DIRECTOR** | HAP OWEN

**DESIGNER/ILLUSTRATOR** | ANNE-MARIE OTVOS

**CLIENT** | JACKSON ZOOLOGICAL PARK

**TOOLS** | WATERCOLOR

**PAPER/PRINTING** | CLASSIC LINEN/OFFSET LITHOGRAPHY

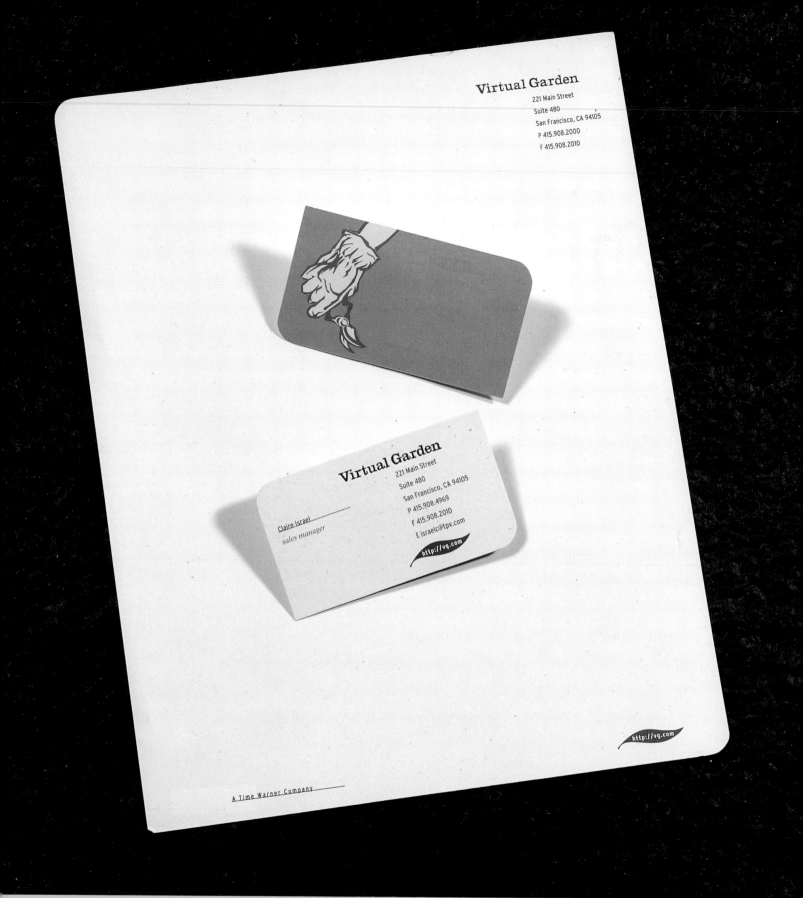

Virtual Garden

221 Main Street
Suite 480
San Francisco, CA 94105
P 415.908.2000
F 415.908.2010

Virtual Garden

221 Main Street
Suite 480
San Francisco, CA 94105
P 415.908.4969
F 415.908.2010
E israelc@tpv.com

Claire Israel
sales manager

http://vg.com

http://vg.com

A Time Warner Company

DESIGN FIRM | THARP DID IT
ART DIRECTOR | RICK THARP
DESIGNERS | RICK THARP, NICOLE COLEMAN
ILLUSTRATOR | RIK OLSON
CLIENT | TIME WARNER
TOOLS | INK, MACINTOSH
PAPER/PRINTING | SIMPSON EVERGREEN/SIMON PRINTING

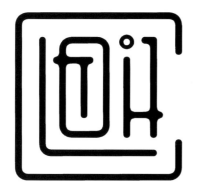

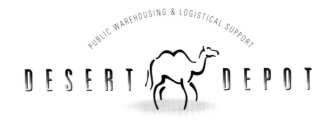

DESIGN FIRM | INSIGHT DESIGN COMMUNICATIONS
ALL DESIGN | SHERRIE AND TRACY HOLDEMAN
CLIENT | CLOTIA WOOD + METAL WORKS
TOOLS | POWER MACINTOSH, MACROMEDIA FREEHAND,
ADOBE PHOTOSHOP

DESIGN FIRM | LORENZ ADVERTISING & DESIGN
ART DIRECTORS | BRIAN LORENZ, ARNE RATERMANIS
DESIGNERS | ARNE RATERMANIS, BRIAN LORENZ
ILLUSTRATOR | ARNE RATERMANIS
CLIENT | DESERT DEPOT
TOOLS | MACINTOSH, ADOBE ILLUSTRATOR
PAPER/PRINTING | CLASSIC CREST/THREE COLOR OFFSET

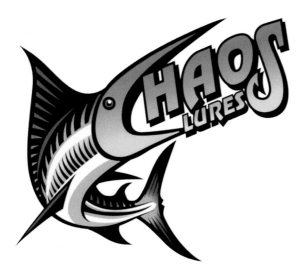

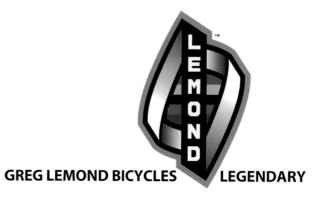

DESIGN FIRM | MIRES DESIGN
ART DIRECTOR/DESIGNER | JOSÉ A. SERRANO
ILLUSTRATOR | TRACY SABIN
CLIENT | CHAOS LURES

DESIGN FIRM | HANSON/DODGE DESIGN
ART DIRECTOR | JOE SUTTER
DESIGNER | SHAWN DOYLE
ILLUSTRATOR | JACK HARGREAVES
CLIENT | TREK BICYCLE CORPORATION
TOOLS | ADOBE ILLUSTRATOR

DESIGN FIRM | SAGMEISTER, INC.

ART DIRECTOR | STEFAN SAGMEISTER

DESIGNERS | STEFAN SAGMEISTER, PATRICK DAILY

ILLUSTRATOR | PATRICK DAILY

CLIENT | SCHERTLER AUDIO TRANSDUCERS

TOOLS | MACINTOSH

PAPER/PRINTING | STRATHMORE WRITING 25% COTTON

DESIGN FIRM | GRETEMAN GROUP

ART DIRECTORS/DESIGNERS | SONIA GRETEMAN, JAMES STRANGE

ILLUSTRATOR | JAMES STRANGE

CLIENT | GRANT TELEGRAPH CENTRE

TOOLS | MACROMEDIA FREEHAND

PAPER/PRINTING | ASTRO PARCHMENT, SAND +

CONFETTI SABLE BLACK/OFFSET

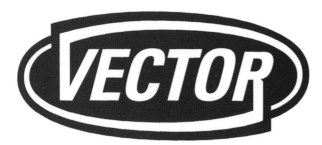

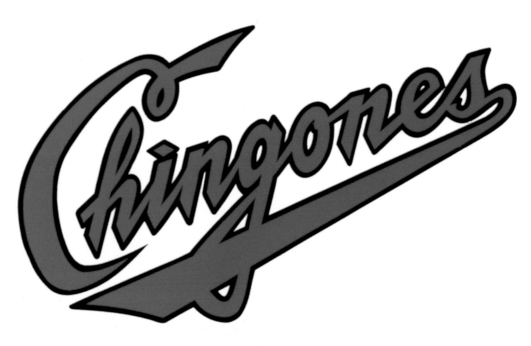

DESIGN FIRM | HANSON/DODGE DESIGN
ART DIRECTOR/DESIGNER | ANIA WASILEWSKA
ILLUSTRATOR | JACK HARGREAVES
CLIENT | VECTOR TECHNOLOGIES, INC.
TOOLS | ADOBE ILLUSTRATOR

DESIGN FIRM | MIRES DESIGN
ART DIRECTOR/DESIGNER | JOSÉ A. SERRANO
PHOTOGRAPHER | CARL VANDERSCHUIT
CLIENT | AGASSI ENTERPRISES

DESIGN FIRM | MIRES DESIGN
ART DIRECTOR/DESIGNER | JOSÉ A. SERRANO
ILLUSTRATOR | TRACY SABIN
CLIENT | CHINGONES

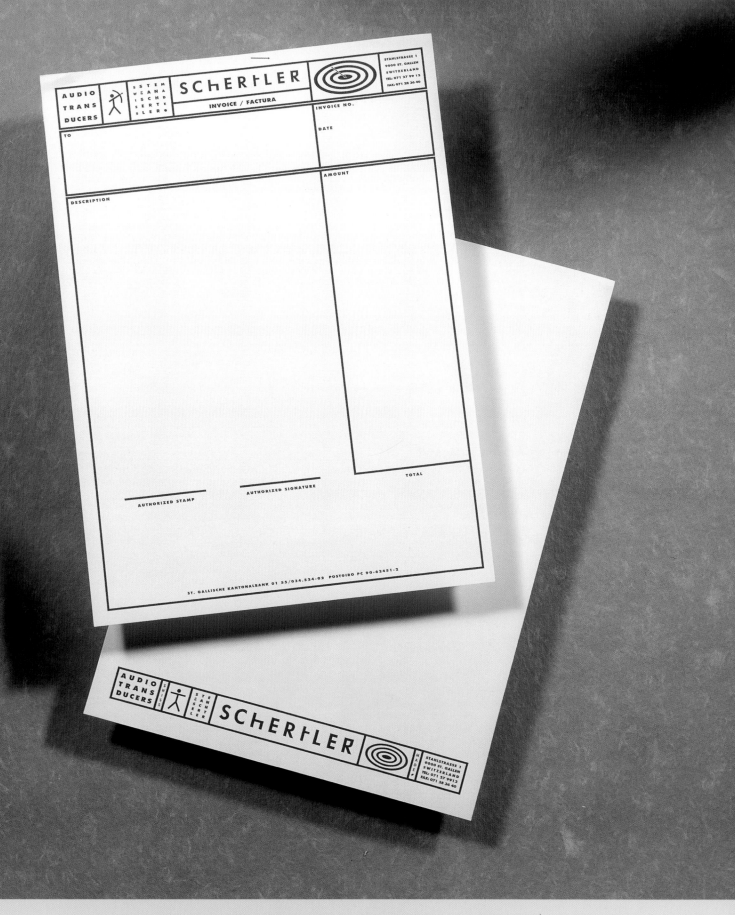

DESIGN FIRM | SAGMEISTER, INC.

ART DIRECTOR | STEFAN SAGMEISTER

DESIGNERS | STEFAN SAGMEISTER, VERONICA OH

PHOTOGRAPHY | MICHAEL GRIMM, STOCK

CLIENT | TOTO

TOOLS | MACINTOSH, 2 1/4 CAMERA

PAPER/PRINTING | STRATHMORE WRITING 25% COTTON

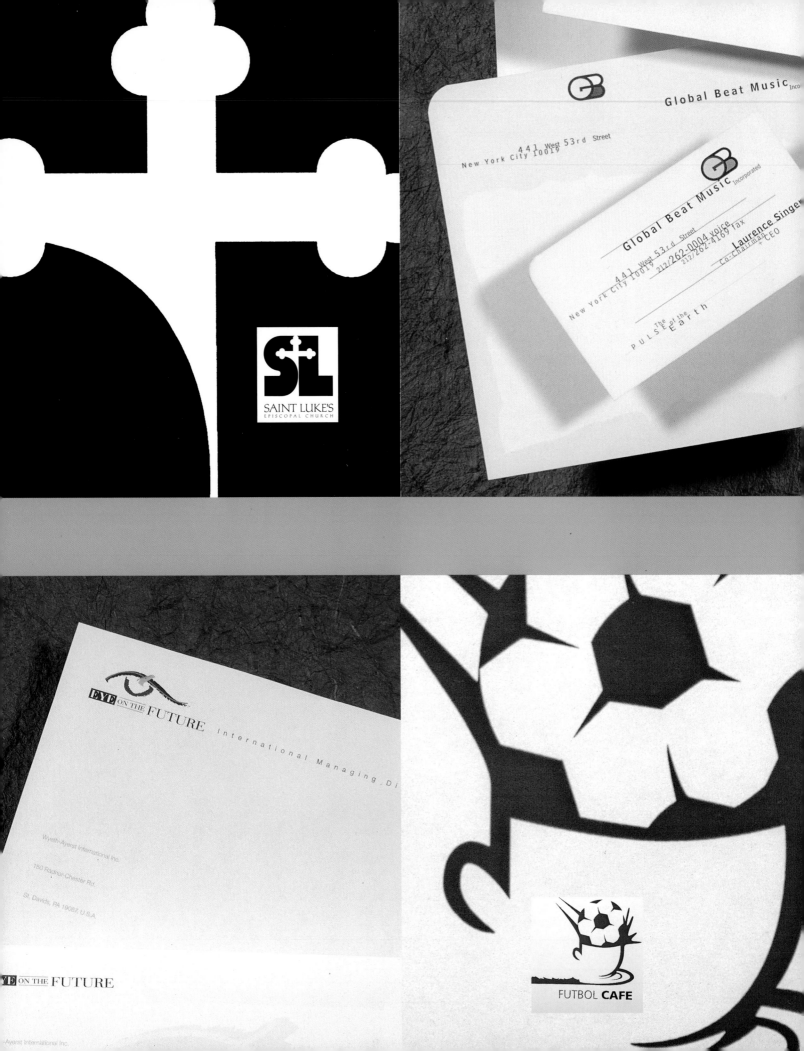

**SₜL**
SAINT LUKE'S
EPISCOPAL CHURCH

Global Beat Music Inc.

441 West 53rd Street
New York City 10019

Global Beat Music Incorporated

441 West 53rd Street
New York City 10019
212/262-0004 voice
212/262-4169 fax

Laurence Singer
Co-Chairman + CEO

The PULSE of the Earth

EYE ON THE FUTURE International Managing Di

Wyeth-Ayerst International Inc.

150 Radnor-Chester Rd.

St. Davids, PA 19087 U.S.A.

EYE ON THE FUTURE

FUTBOL CAFE

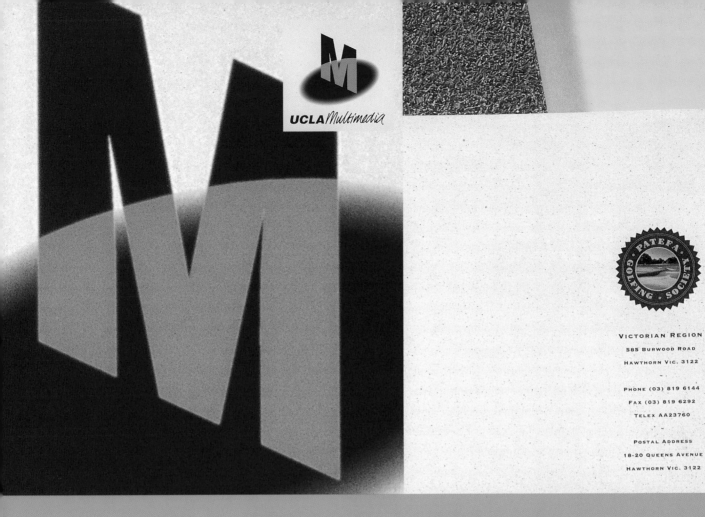

UCLA *Multimedia*

PATEFA GOLFING SOCIETY

Victorian Region
585 Burwood Road
Hawthorn Vic. 3122

~

Phone (03) 819 6144
Fax (03) 819 6292
Telex AA23760

~

Postal Address
18-20 Queens Avenue
Hawthorn Vic. 3122

# Miscellaneous

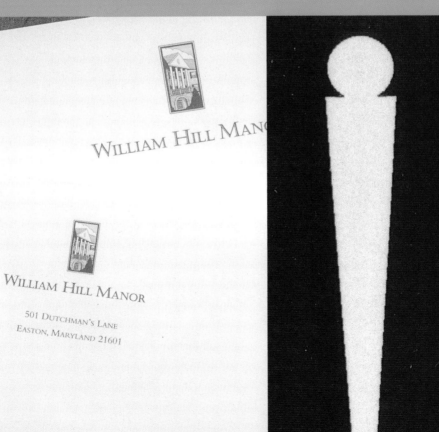

WILLIAM HILL MANOR

WILLIAM HILL MANOR

501 Dutchman's Lane
Easton, Maryland 21601

JOSEPH & EDNA
JOSEPHSON
INSTITUTE
OF ETHICS

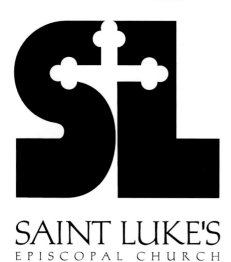

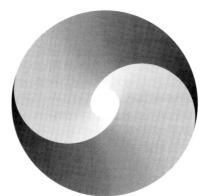

DESIGN FIRM | THE WELLER INSTITUTE
ALL DESIGN | DON WELLER
CLIENT | SAINT LUKE'S EPISCOPAL CHURCH
TOOLS | ADOBE ILLUSTRATOR, QUARKXPRESS

DESIGN FIRM | WITHERSPOON ADVERTISING
CREATIVE DIRECTOR | DEBRA MORROW
ART DIRECTOR/DESIGNER | RANDY PADORR-BLACK
ILLUSTRATOR | JAMES MELLARD
CLIENT | WOUND HEALING & HYPERBARIC MEDICINE CENTER

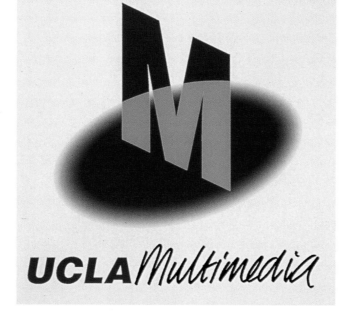

DESIGN FIRM | SHIMOKOCHI/REEVES
ART DIRECTOR | MAMORU SHIMOKOCHI, ANNE REEVES
CLIENT | UCLA MULTIMEDIA
TOOLS | ADOBE ILLUSTRATOR

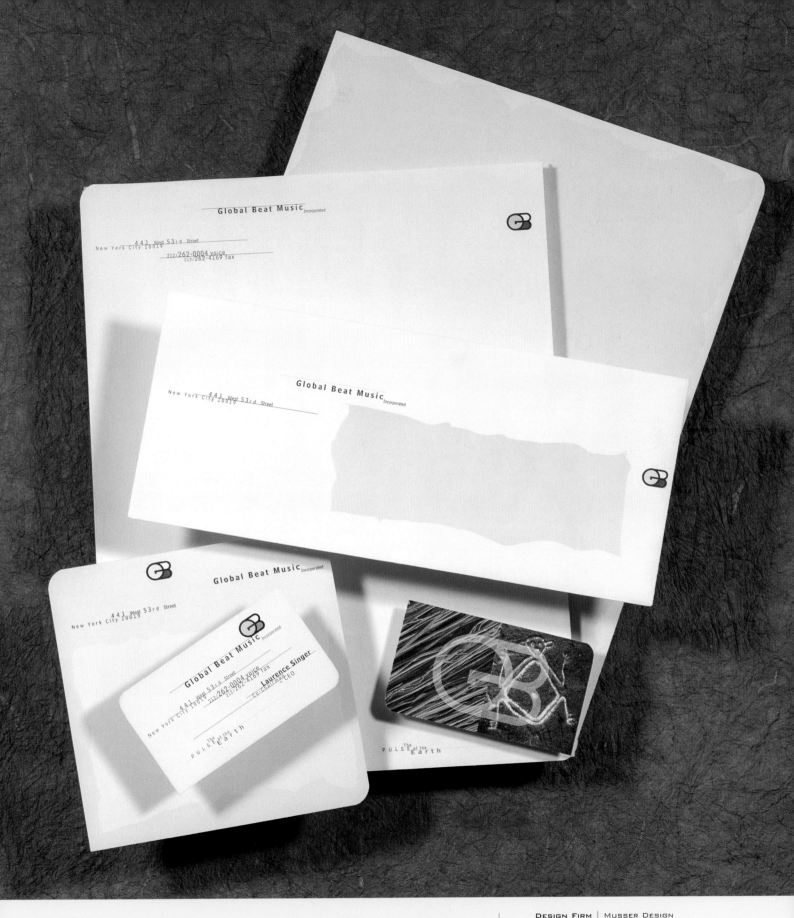

DESIGN FIRM | MUSSER DESIGN
ART DIRECTOR/DESIGNER | JERRY KING MUSSER
CLIENT | GLOBAL BEAT MEDIA
TOOLS | ADOBE ILLUSTRATOR

DESIGN FIRM | AFTER HOURS CREATIVE

ART DIRECTOR/DESIGNER | AFTER HOURS CREATIVE

PHOTOGRAPHER | ART HOLEMAN

CLIENT | CULINARY ARTS & ENTERTAINMENT

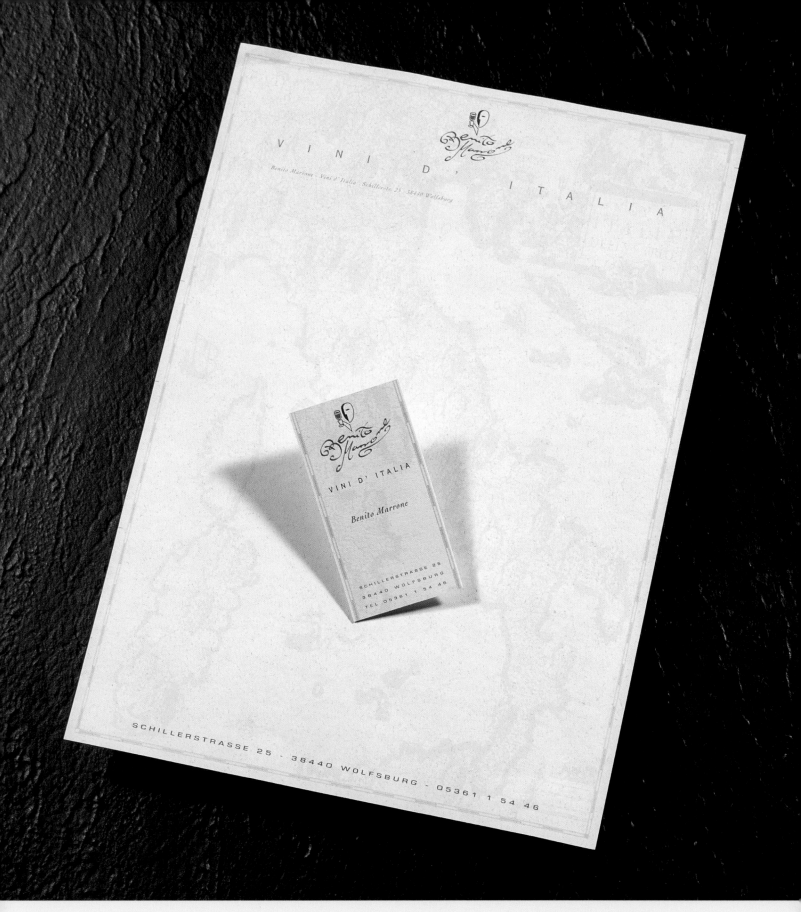

DESIGN FIRM | VOSS DESIGN
ART DIRECTOR/DESIGNER | AXEL VOSS
CLIENT | BENITO MARRONE
PAPER/PRINTING | COUNTRYSIDE

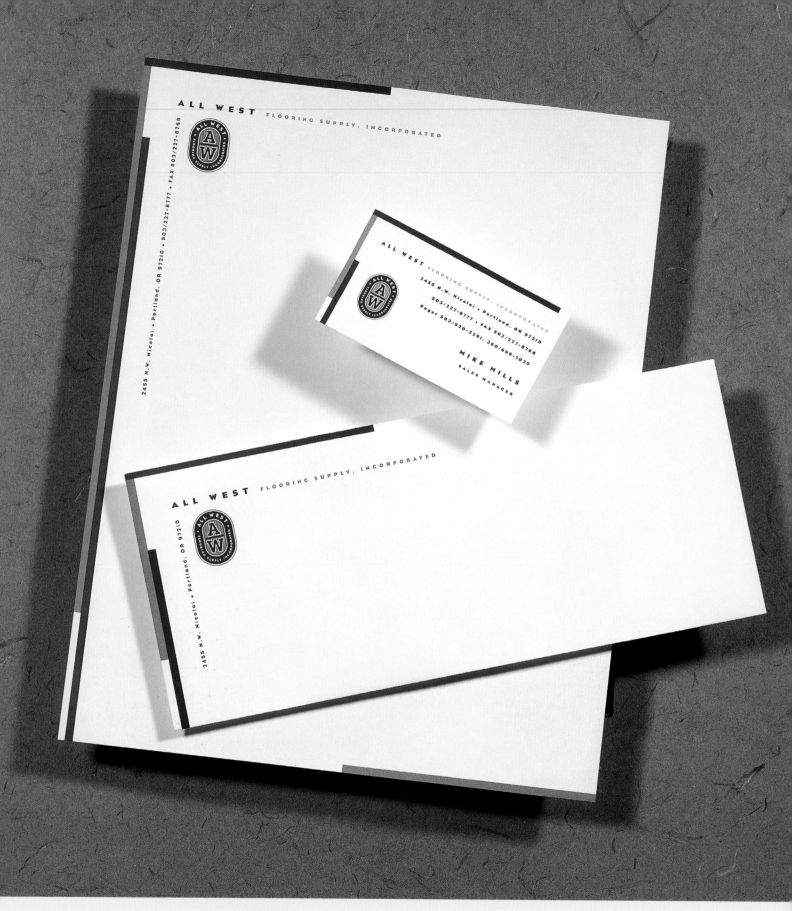

DESIGN FIRM | ROBERT BAILEY INCORPORATED

ART DIRECTOR | CONNIE LIGHTNER

DESIGNERS | CONNIE LIGHTNER, DAN FRANKLIN

CLIENT | ALL WEST FLOORING SUPPLY, INC.

TOOLS | MACROMEDIA FREEHAND, QUARKXPRESS

PAPER/PRINTING | PROTOCOL RECYCLED BRIGHT

WHITE/CNS GRAPHICS

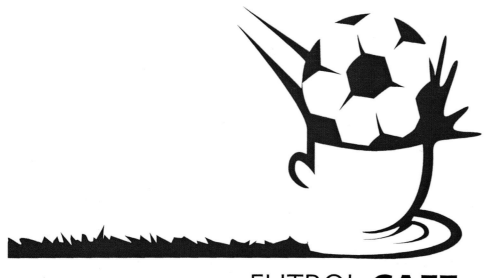

FUTBOL **CAFE**

DESIGN FIRM | CATO BERRO DISEÑO
ART DIRECTOR | GONZALO BERRO
DESIGNER | GONZALO BERRO/ESTEBAN SERRANO
ILLUSTRATOR | ESTEBAN SERRANO
CLIENT | FUTBOL CAFE/BAR
TOOLS | ADOBE ILLUSTRATOR

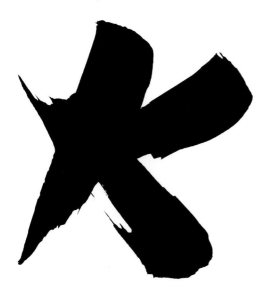

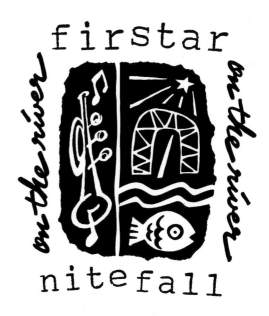

DESIGN FIRM | MICHAEL STANARD DESIGN, INC.
ART DIRECTOR | MICHAEL STANARD
DESIGNER/ILLUSTRATOR | MICHAEL STANARD, DEV HOMSI
CLIENT | NORTHWESTERN UNIVERSITY

DESIGN FIRM | SAYLES GRAPHIC DESIGN
ALL DESIGN | JOHN SAYLES
CLIENT | DES MOINES PARK & RECREATION DEPT.

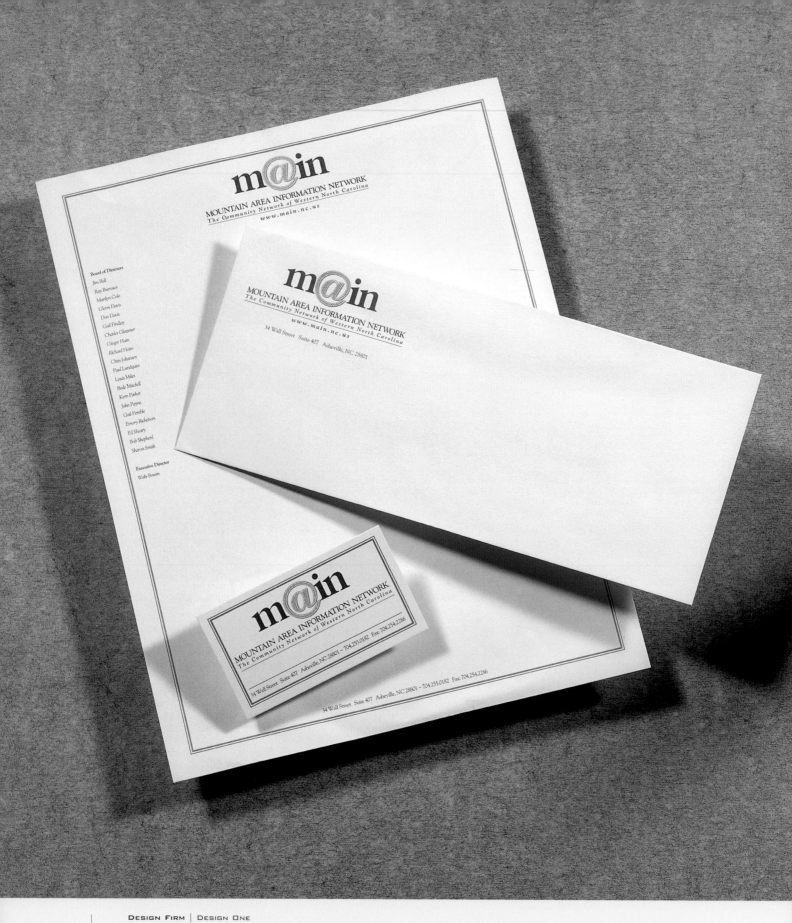

DESIGN FIRM | DESIGN ONE

DESIGNER | LYN FRANKLIN

CLIENT | MAIN

AUSTRALIAN TRANSPORT MANAGEMENT

ATM logistic solutions

AUSTRALIAN TRANSPORT MANAGEMENT PTY LTD • ACN 069 426 884

48 Elizabeth Street West Meadows Victoria Australia 3049

POSTAL ADDRESS: PO Box 745 Tullamarine Victoria 3043

TELEPHONE: 0419 334 563 • FACSIMILE: 03 9338 4894

DESIGN FIRM | MAMMOLITI CHAN DESIGN

ART DIRECTOR | TONY MAMMOLITI

DESIGNERS | CHWEE KUAN CHAN, TONY MAMMOLITI

ILLUSTRATOR | CHWEE KUAN CHAN

CLIENT | AUSTRALIAN TRANSPORT MANAGEMENT

PAPER/PRINTING | ONE PMS ON PARCHMENT STOCK

SPRING
HOLLOW

2750 S. 875 E ⬦ Zionsville, IN ⬦ 46077.9526 ⬦ 317.769.6839

DESIGN FIRM | HELD DIEDRICH

ART DIRECTOR | DOUG DIEDRICH

DESIGNER/ILLUSTRATOR | MEGAN SNOW

CLIENT | SPRING HOLLOW

TOOLS | QUARKXPRESS, ADOBE ILLUSTRATOR

PAPER/PRINTING | NEENAH, CLASSIC LAID,

NATURAL WHITE, LASER FINISH/OFFSET

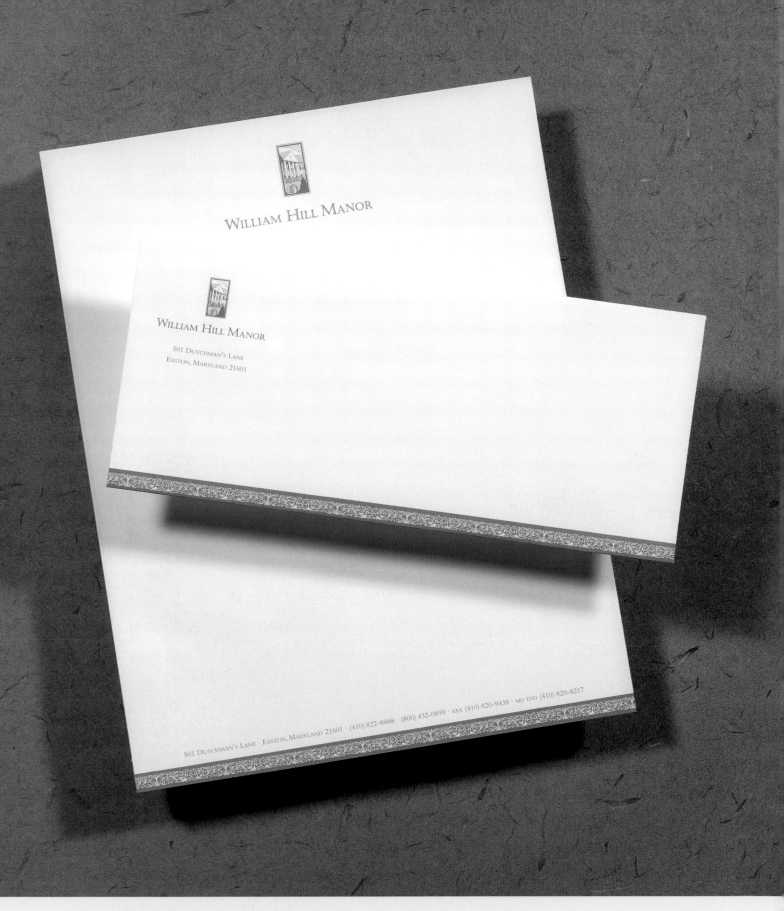

**WILLIAM HILL MANOR**

**WILLIAM HILL MANOR**

501 DUTCHMAN'S LANE
EASTON, MARYLAND 21601

501 DUTCHMAN'S LANE · EASTON, MARYLAND 21601 · (410) 822-8888 · (800) 432-0899 · FAX (410) 820-9438 · MD TDD (410) 820-8217

DESIGN FIRM | WHITNEY EDWARDS DESIGN

ALL DESIGN | CHARLENE WHITNEY EDWARDS

CLIENT | WILLIAM HILL MANOR

TOOLS | ADOBE PHOTOSHOP, ADOBE ILLUSTRATOR,
QUARKXPRESS

PAPER/PRINTING | CRANES/ONE COLOR

VICTORIAN REGION
585 BURWOOD ROAD
HAWTHORN VIC. 3122

PHONE (03) 819 6144
FAX (03) 819 6292
TELEX AA23760

POSTAL ADDRESS
18-20 QUEENS AVENUE
HAWTHORN VIC. 3122

DESIGN FIRM | WATTS GRAPHIC DESIGN
ART DIRECTORS/DESIGNERS | HELEN AND PETER WATTS
CLIENT | PATEFA GOLFING SOCIETY

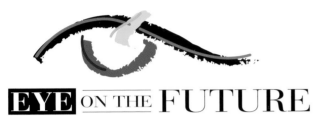

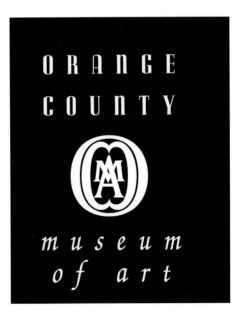

DESIGN FIRM | MUELLER & WISTER, INC.
ALL DESIGN | JOSEPH M. DELICH
CLIENT | WYETH-AYERST INTERNATIONAL
TOOLS | ADOBE PHOTOSHOP, STREAMLINE, MACROMEDIA FREEHAND

DESIGN FIRM | ARMINDA HOPKINS & ASSOCIATES
ART DIRECTOR/DESIGNER | MELANIE MATSON
CLIENT | FREDONIA HEALTH SYSTEMS
TOOLS | QUARKXPRESS, ADOBE ILLUSTRATOR

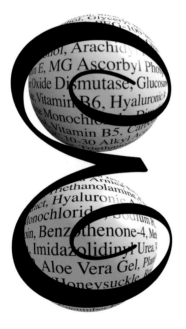

DESIGN FIRM | LOVE PACKAGING GROUP
ALL DESIGN | BRIAN MILLER
CLIENT | ELOGEN, INC.
TOOLS | MACROMEDIA FREEHAND, ADOBE PHOTOSHOP

DESIGN FIRM | MIKE SALISBURY COMMUNICATIONS, INC.
ART DIRECTOR | MIKE SALISBURY
DESIGNER | MARY EVELYN MCGOUGH
ILLUSTRATOR | BOB MAILE
CLIENT | ORANGE COUNTY MUSEUM OF ART

# CATHEDRAL OF ST. PETER IN CHAINS

325 West Eighth Street / Cincinnati, Ohio  45202 - 1977 / Phone: 513 - 421 - 5354 / Fax: 513 - 241 - 9517

DESIGN FIRM | WOOD/BROD DESIGN

ART DIRECTOR/DESIGNER | STAN BROD

CLIENT | CATHEDRAL OF ST. PETER IN CHAINS

TOOLS | ADOBE ILLUSTRATOR

PAPER/PRINTING | STRATHMORE/HENNEGAN COMPANY

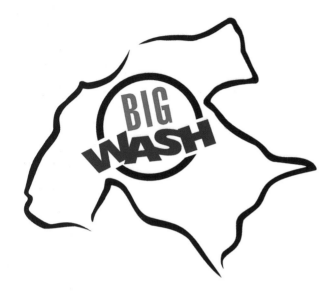

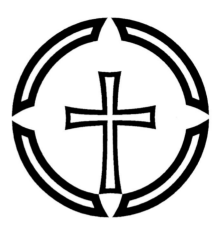

DESIGN FIRM | CLARK DESIGN
ART DIRECTOR | ANNEMARIE CLARK
DESIGNER | CRAIG STOUT
CLIENT | HOPE HOUSING/BIG WASH
TOOLS | ADOBE ILLUSTRATOR

DESIGN FIRM | RICK EIBER DESIGN (RED)
ART DIRECTOR/DESIGNER | RICK EIBER
CLIENT | COLUMBIA BAPTIST CONFERENCE
TOOLS | ADOBE ILLUSTRATOR

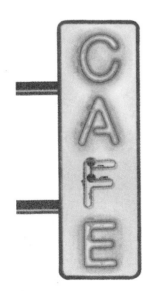

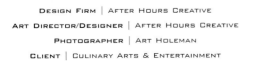

DESIGN FOR THE FUTURE AND
3RD ANNUAL LEARNING CONFERENCE

DESIGN FIRM | AFTER HOURS CREATIVE
ART DIRECTOR/DESIGNER | AFTER HOURS CREATIVE
PHOTOGRAPHER | ART HOLEMAN
CLIENT | CULINARY ARTS & ENTERTAINMENT

DESIGN FIRM | CECILY ROBERTS DESIGN
ALL DESIGN | CECILY ROBERTS
CLIENT | KAISER PERMANENTE/DESIGN FOR THE FUTURE CONFERENCE
TOOLS | MACROMEDIA FREEHAND, QUARKXPRESS

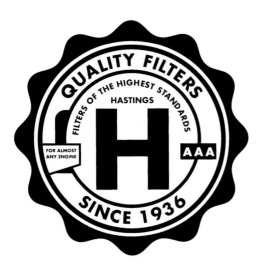

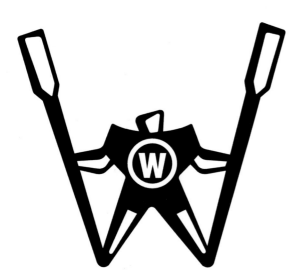

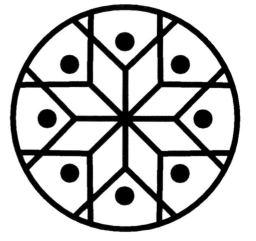

DESIGN FIRM | INSIGHT DESIGN COMMUNICATIONS
ALL DESIGN | SHERRIE AND TRACY HOLDEMAN
CLIENT | WORLD FITNESS, INC.
TOOLS | MACROMEDIA FREEHAND

DESIGN FIRM | CHRIS ST. CYR GRAPHIC DESIGN
ART DIRECTOR/DESIGNER | CHRIS ST. CYR
CLIENT | STREET PROJECT BOSTON
TOOLS | ADOBE PHOTOSHOP, QUARKXPRESS

DESIGN FIRM | LOVE PACKAGING GROUP
ALL DESIGN | BRIAN MILLER
CLIENT | WICHITA STATE UNIVERSITY, MEN'S CREW TEAM
TOOLS | MACROMEDIA FREEHAND

DESIGN FIRM | RICK EIBER DESIGN (RED)
ART DIRECTOR/DESIGNER | RICK EIBER
CLIENT | COLUMBIA BAPTIST CONFERENCE
TOOLS | ADOBE ILLUSTRATOR
PAPER/PRINTING | CURTIS BRIGHTWATER/TWO COLOR OVER TWO COLOR

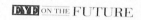

**EYE** ON THE **FUTURE** · International Managing Directors' Meeting

Wyeth-Ayerst International Inc.

150 Radnor-Chester Rd.

St. Davids, PA 19087, U.S.A.

**EYE** ON THE **FUTURE**

Wyeth-Ayerst International Inc.

150 Radnor-Chester Rd.

St. Davids, PA 19087, U.S.A.

DESIGN FIRM | MUELLER & WISTER, INC.

ALL DESIGN | JOSEPH DELICH

CLIENT | WYETH-AYERST INTERNATIONAL, INC.

TOOLS | ADOBE ILLUSTRATOR

DESIGN FIRM | PARHAM SANTANA, INC.

ART DIRECTOR/DESIGNER | RICK TESORO

CLIENT | PROJECT FOR PUBLIC SPACES

PAPER/PRINTING | LETTERHEAD & ENVELOPE: STARWHITE

VICKSBURG TIARA 70 LB., BUSINESS CARD: STARWHITE

VICKSBURG TIARA 130 LB. DOUBLE COVER, LABEL:

BROWNBRIDGE WHITE ULTRA-MATTE CRACK N PEEL

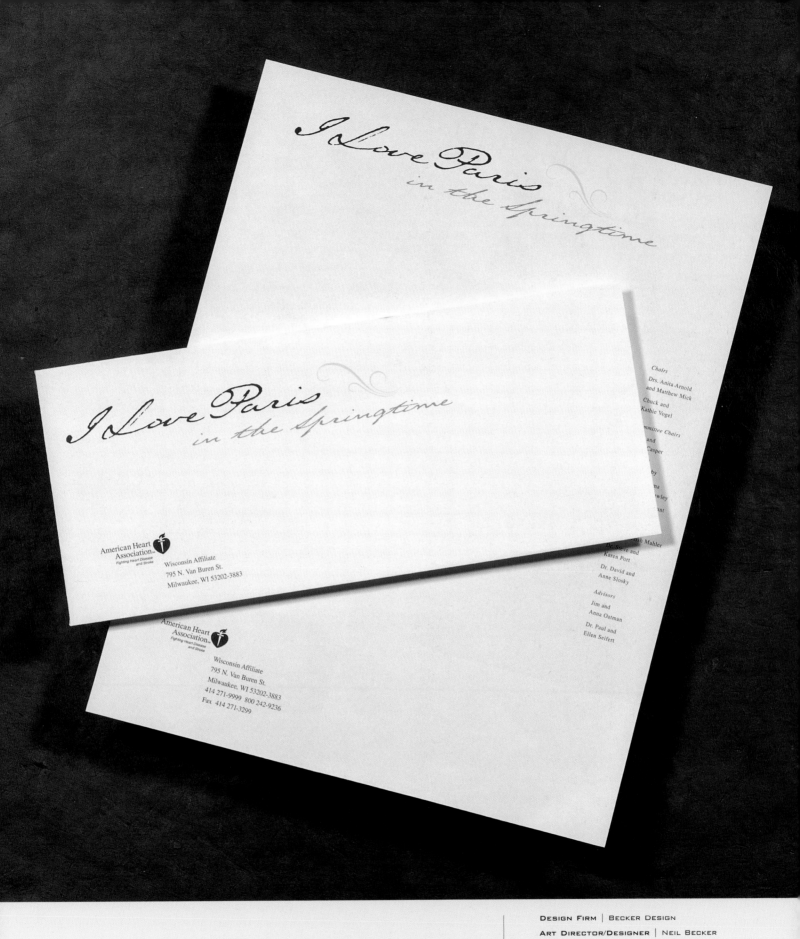

DESIGN FIRM | BECKER DESIGN

ART DIRECTOR/DESIGNER | NEIL BECKER

CLIENT | AMERICAN HEART ASSOCIATION

TOOLS | QUARKXPRESS, ADOBE ILLUSTRATOR

PAPER/PRINTING | NEENAH CLASSIC CREST RECYCLED

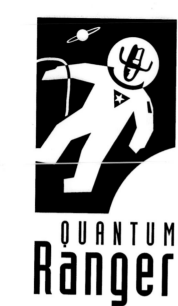

QUANTUM
Ranger

DESIGN FIRM | DESIGN CENTER
ART DIRECTOR | JOHN REGER
DESIGNER | CORY DOCKEN
CLIENT | SCIMED

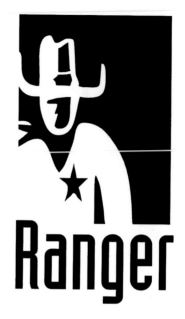

Ranger

DESIGN FIRM | DESIGN CENTER
ART DIRECTOR | JOHN REGER
DESIGNER | CORY DOCKEN
CLIENT | SCIMED

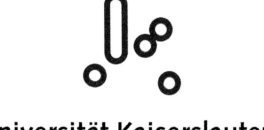

# Universität Kaiserslautern

DESIGN FIRM | GEFFERT DESIGN
DESIGNER | GERALD GEFFERT
CLIENT | UNIVERSITÄT KAISERSLAUTERN

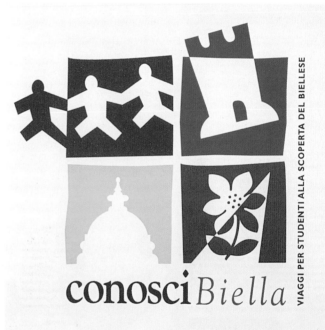

conosci Biella

VIAGGI PER STUDENTI ALLA SCOPERTA DEL BIELLESE

DESIGN FIRM | IMPRESS SAS
CLIENT | PROVINCIA DI BIELLA

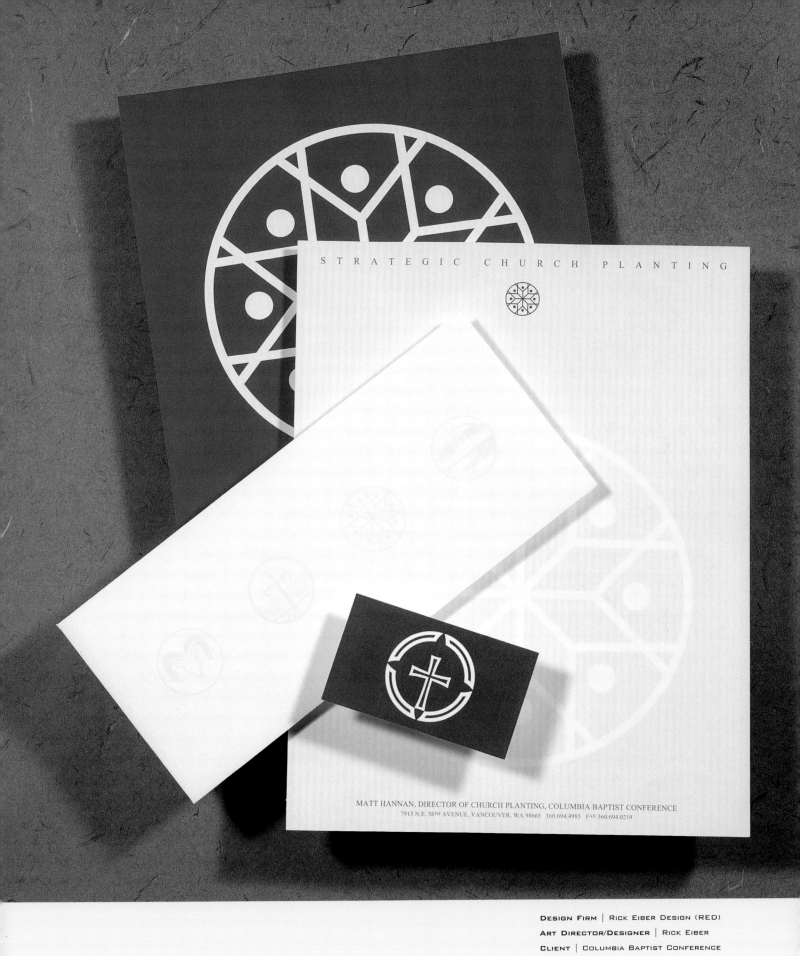

STRATEGIC CHURCH PLANTING

MATT HANNAN, DIRECTOR OF CHURCH PLANTING, COLUMBIA BAPTIST CONFERENCE
7913 N.E. 58TH AVENUE, VANCOUVER, WA 98665   360.694.4985   FAX 360.694.0219

DESIGN FIRM | RICK EIBER DESIGN (RED)

ART DIRECTOR/DESIGNER | RICK EIBER

CLIENT | COLUMBIA BAPTIST CONFERENCE

TOOLS | ADOBE ILLUSTRATOR

PAPER/PRINTING | CURTIS BRIGHTWATER/TWO

COLOR OVER TWO COLOR

# INDEX AND DIRECTORY

DESIGN CENTER 27, 65, 186
15119 Minnetonka Boulevard
Minnetonka, MN 55345

DESIGN INFINITUM 117
9540 NW Engleman Street
Portland, OR 97229-9130

DESIGN ONE 174
26 1/2 Battery Park Avenue
Asheville, NC 28801

DRUVI ART AND DESIGN 90
8200 Wisconsin Avenue, Suite 1607
Bethesda, MD 20814

DOGSTAR 29, 45, 65, 121
626 54th Street South
Birmingham, AL 35212

DUCK SOUP GRAPHICS, INC. 140
257 Grand Meadow Crescent
Edmonton, AL T6L IW9
Canada

E. CHRISTOPHER KLUMB ASSOCIATES, INC. 43
260 Norton
Darien, CT 06820

ELENA DESIGN 38
3024 Old Orchard Lane
Bedford, TX 76021

EYE DESIGN INCORPORATED 36
8180 Greensboro Drive, #180
McLean, VA 22102

FAIA DESIGN 143
130 Camino Pacifico
Aptos, CA 95003

FIRE HOUSE, INC. 129
314 North St. Joseph Avenue
Evansville, IN 47712

FLAHERTY ART & DESIGN 127, 136
28 Jackson Street
Quincy, MA 01269

FORDESIGN 74
533 Twin Bridge
Alexandria, LA 71303

FRCH DESIGN WORLDWIDE 127, 146
Graphic Design Society, Inc.
444 North Front Street, #211
Columbus, OH 43215

GAF ADVERTISING DESIGN 77
7215 Holly Hill #102
Dallas, TX 75231

GASOLINE GRAPHIC DESIGN 88
5704 College Avenue
Des Moines, IA 50310

GEFFERT DESIGN 186
Eichendorffstrasse 6
31135 Hildesheim
Germany

GET SMART DESIGN COMPANY 36, 74
899 Jackson Street
Dubuque, IA 52001

GILLIS & SMILER 25, 59
1105 Glendon Avenue
Los Angeles, CA 90024

GRAND DESIGN COMPANY 30, 33
1902 Valley Centre 80-82
Morrison Hill Road
Hong Kong

GRAY CAT DESIGN 97, 102
920 N. Franklin, Suite 303
Chicago, IL 60610

GRETEMAN GROUP 163
142 N. Mosley
Wichita, KS 67202

HANSON/DODGE DESIGN 154, 157, 164
301 N. Water Street
Milwaukee, WI 53202

HELD DIEDRICH 176
703 East 30th Street, Suite 16
Indianapolis, IN 46205

HIEROGLYPHICS ART & DESIGN 113
602 E. Grove Street
Mishawaka, IN 46545

HORNALL ANDERSON DESIGN WORKS, INC.
28, 99, 151, 153
1008 Western Avenue, Suite 600
Seattle, WA 98104

ICEHOUSE DESIGN 37, 47, 126
135 West Elm Street
New Haven, CT 06515

IMAGINE THAT, INC. 17
1676 Oak Street
Washington, DC 20010

IMPRESS SAS 186
Via Galimberti 18
13051 Biella
Italy

NAGORNY DESIGN 88
10675 Charles Plaza, Suite 930
Omaha, NE 68114

NESNADNY + SCHWARTZ 63
10803 Magnolia Drive
Cleveland, OH 44106

OAKLEY DESIGN STUDIOS 97
519 SE Park Avenue
Suite 521
Portland, OR 97205

ON THE EDGE 133, 135, 141, 145
505 30th Street, Suite 211
Newport Beach, CA 92663

PARHAM SANTANA, INC. 184
7 West 18TH Street
7TH Floor
New York, NY 10011

PENCIL NECK PRODUCTIONS 25
2513 Lands End Road
Carrolton, TX 75006

PHILLIPS DESIGN GROUP 119
25 Drydock Avenue
Boston, MA 02210

PHOENIX CREATIVE 33, 80
611 North Tenth
St. Louis, MO 63101

PLATINUM DESIGN, INC. 96
14 West 23 Street
New York, NY 10010

THE PROVEN EDGE 130, 132
12616 D Springbrook Drive
San Diego, CA 92128

RAMONA HUTKO DESIGN 46
4712 South Chelsea Lane
Bethesda, MD 20814

REDGRAFIX DESIGN & ILLUSTRATION 89
19750 West Observatory Road
New Berlin, WI 53146

RICK EIBER DESIGN (RED) 20, 23, 181,
182, 187
31014 SE 58th Street
Preston, WA 98050

RICK SEALOCK 106
#2 217 10th Avenue SW
Calgary, AL T2R 0A4
Canada

ROBERT BAILEY INCORPORATED 25, 172
0121 SW Bancroft Street
Portland, OR 97201

SAGMEISTER, INC. 13, 26, 158, 165
222 West 14 Street #15A
New York, NY 10011

S&N DESIGN 136
121 North 8th Street
Manhattan, KS 66502

"SAY AH!" CREATIVE 103, 121
PO Box 8005, 515 Broad Street
Menasha, WI 54952

SAYLES GRAPHIC DESIGN 41, 52, 71, 125,
128, 136, 162, 173
308 Eighth Street
Des Moines, IA 50309

SHIMOKOCHI/REEVES 10, 18, 168
4465 Wilshire Boulevard, #305
Los Angeles, CA 90010

SIBLEY/PETEET DESIGN 108, 116
3232 McKinney, Suite 1200
Dallas, TX 75204

SOMMESE DESIGN 142
481 Glenn Road
State College, PA 16803

SPACE DESIGN INTERNATIONAL 81
Graphic Design Society, Inc.
444 North Front Street
Suite 211
Columbus, OH 43215

STEFAN DZIALLAS DESIGN 35
Olbersstrasse 9
D-28307 Bremen
Germany

STEWART MONDERER DESIGN, INC. 81
10 Thatcher Street, Suite 112
Boston, MA 02113

STORM DESIGN & ADVERTISING CONSULTANCY
15, 92, 121
174 Albert Street
Prahran 3181, Victoria
Australia

SULLIVAN PERKINS 12, 61
2811 McKinney, Suite 320 LBIII
Dallas, TX 75204

SUSAN GUERRA DESIGN 85, 101
30 Gray Street
Montclair, NJ 07042

SWIETER DESIGN 54
3227 McKinney Avenue, Suite 201
Dallas, TX 75204